Libraries   A Briefing and Design Guide

LIBRARIES

First published in 1986 by the Architectural Press Ltd,
9 Queen Anne's Gate, London SW1H 9BY

BRITISH LIBRARY CATALOGUING IN PUBLICATION DATA

Konya, Allan
    Libraries: a briefing and design guide.
    1. Library architecture   2. Architecture
    – Designs and plans
    I. Title
    727'.8   Z679

    ISBN 0–85139–765–4

Typeset by Crawley Composition Ltd, Crawley
Printed and bound in Great Britain by Biddles Ltd,
Guildford and King's Lynn

Acknowledgements

The development of this rather ambitious series of books – first suggested by Maritz Vandenberg (then the Commissioning Editor for Architectural Press Books) in April 1979 – has been a long and tiring process, and would not have reached its present stage without the continuous support and encouragement given by Maritz and his colleagues throughout these years.

Although inspired by the series of 'Briefing and Design Guides' which appeared in *The Architects' Journal* during the 1960s, the format has been revised and the contents completely rewritten and updated. The author is indebted to a number of people for their help, in particular Mike Jenks of the Department of Architecture at Oxford Polytechnic; Dr Frank Duffy of DEGW (Architects and Space Planners) for reading and re-reading parts of the manuscript, for offering invaluable criticism and advice, and for providing useful reference material; Professor Henry Sanoff (author of *Methods of Architectural Programming*) for reading the introduction and making suggestions for improvements; Mr Bob Williams of the College of Librarianship Wales for his good many hours of labour on my behalf; Professors Alewyn Burger and Dieter Holm for their help with defining the problem at the start of the project; *The Architects' Journal* for permission to reproduce photographs in Appendix 3; and last but not least, Dorothy Pontin and her assistants in the Architectural Press library for finding so much of the reference material that was needed.

Thanks must go to a number of the specialist manufacturers of library equipment who generously provided a large number of photographs and to the following institutions for their assistance with information: The Library Association library, The Royal Institution of Chartered Surveyors, The British Institute of Interior Design and The Landscape Institute.

Contents

Introduction

1.   Who is this book for?

The main purpose of these *Briefing and Design Guides* is to provide all those involved in the initial stages of the building process – clients, users and members of the design team – with a set of tools. These tools, or resources, will help them communicate more effectively so that they are able to work together to develop rich design briefs which will, it is hoped, culminate in the best solutions to their particular problems.

There are a few points to be stressed. First, for every building within each major type covered by this series there is a wide range of variables: the building may be large or small, simple or complex; the client may be a public body, a large private organisation or a small firm, a family or an individual; those involved may be experienced or inexperienced in building; the design team may be big or small, may or may not have experience with the relevant building type; and every team will have its individual method of working. It is impossible to cover all the likely combinations and to provide an ideal set of guidelines for all clients, users and designers in all situations. There will obviously, therefore, tend to be a bias in these *Guides* towards a particular briefing context that is not the most simple nor the most complex, but rather a fairly uncomplicated middle range. In spite of this it should be possible to use each *Guide*, if one realises and accepts its limitations, as a basic tool not only for the simplest but also for the most complex of projects.

Secondly, there is no one way of approaching the design process – and this is also true of briefing. Procedures will vary, for example, between those used by and for different types of client, and by and for the public and private sectors. Although the contents of each *Guide* are organised and presented in a specific linear sequence, as demonstrated in Fig. 0.1, they should not be seen or used as a rigid set of sequential instructions but rather as a loose framework, or flexible tool, which can be adapted to suit individual requirements.

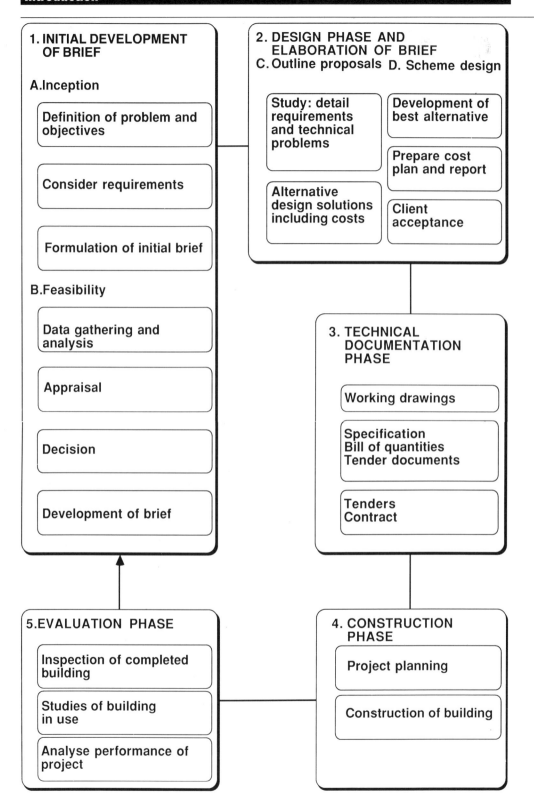

Fig. 0.1 *The main phases and steps of the complete briefing and design process. This book is specifically concerned with phases 1 and 2. (Based on stages A to D of 'Plan of Work'; see Appendix A.1.a.)*

Thirdly, the guidance contained in these books is intended for the main participants in the process of briefing and design, but it is not always possible to distinguish clearly between that which is, for example, specifically the role of the client, and that which is the responsibility of others. It is not advisable to generalise about who should undertake each and every task: this is something to be determined by those involved in each individual project. Wherever possible, however, an indication is given of who is most likely to be responsible.

2.   What is design?

The design of buildings is, at its simplest, the creative development of an idea – in three-dimensional form – to solve a specific problem. This problem-solving activity is called the 'design process'. This term is generally used to describe everything that happens from the time a problem is first outlined to the finalised design. The methods used can range from those based on intuition and experience on the one hand, to extremely formal and inflexible logical or mathematical approaches on the other. Whether consciously applied or not, virtually all of the procedures will include the following actions in one form or another:

—   recognition and definition of the problem and objectives and consideration of the component sub-problems.

—   observation and collection of data relevant to the problem.

—   analysis of requirements and data collected.

—   development of alternative ideas and solutions. Design can never produce the one correct answer, and from the innumerable possibilities those that seem most suitable for the specific problem will be sought.

—   synthesis, or the putting together of ideas to form complete designs.

—   evaluation, or the testing of alternative designs against requirements, and optimisation.

The process is not a simple linear sequence of logical steps leading neatly from one phase to another – of finding the right answer at each step or phase before progressing to the next – but rather a series of actions comprising steps grouped for convenience into phases, some or all of which may occur simultaneously. As new information becomes available ideas that seemed perfectly adequate at an earlier step or phase may have to be changed. Indeed, the complete cycle of actions may have to be reconsidered several times.

3.   The importance of the brief

In a world of increasing complexity and rapid technological change, the whole process of design and building has become ever more difficult. There has been an increase not only in the number of different types of buildings needed, but also in the size and complexity of projects. The number of alternatives has also increased: more feasible solutions, more materials, systems and technologies available, more experts and specialists, and a greater number of schools of thought than in the past. In addition, there are countless other problems to be contended with: bureaucracy, controls, regulations and standards; new imperatives such as energy conservation and changing social needs; the explosion of information; economic constraints and a growing demand for guaranteed performance-in-use. Also, as the process becomes more involved and susceptible to delays, time becomes a scarcer commodity and developments are expected much faster.

The increasingly complex operations to be performed, the mass of information to be collected, the involvement of many people who have contributions to make, and the number of decisions to be taken in the design of even the simplest of buildings, have all made it more and more difficult to rely on intuition and experience alone. As a result thorough briefing has, in recent years, rightly come to be seen as an integral part of the design process.

4. How to use this book

Each *Guide* covers a major building type. Section 1 is relevant to all projects: it provides an outline description of the briefing process and the main participants and gives detailed guidelines for the initial procedure that is basic to any project. It stands as a checklist for the architect, as well as supplying clients with a framework within which to consider their requirements.

The main body of the text is contained in Section 2. This is specific to the building type and includes aids to concept-selection and basic design information. It is divided into five parts: introduction, inception, feasibility, detailed brief and design. The text is in the form of instructions and checklists with comprehensive source and detail information, and is backed up by the appendices. The first three parts of Section 2 are for all concerned with the briefing/design process. The last two parts are intended mainly for the design team but can usefully be referred to by clients and users so that they are aware of the type of information required by the design team for the later design stages.

SECTION ONE
GENERAL

Introduction

1.1 Buildings

Buildings represent, amongst other things, energy, labour and materials. These either cannot be replaced or can only be replaced at great cost. The severe economic recession, the energy crisis and an awareness that resources are finite have led to the realisation that existing buildings are a valuable commodity to be conserved, regardless of their historic or architectural merits, and in addition, that new buildings must be designed and built to last.

Building development today is increasingly concerned with the recyling of space in one way or another. This may be done by:

— extension or addition to a structure owned by the client to provide more space or new facilities.

— alteration of, or modification to, existing premises, which does not lead to a change of use.

— maintenance or refurbishment of an existing structure to improve its appearance and prolong its life.

— conversion of existing premises involving a change of use, for example, from a warehouse to offices or an hotel.

Conversion and rehabilitation are important not only from the point of view of physical resources, but also as a means of revitalising older, densely built, run-down inner-city areas.

In the case of new work and of many conversion or extension projects, a major goal is to provide a building of 'long life, low energy usage and loose fit' – in other words, to reduce capital turnover by making it continually viable with low fuel and maintenance costs as well as easily adaptable to changing use. On the point of changing use: although it is important to identify and design for the specific users, there is an increasing emphasis on flexibility so that the building created will be adaptable to the extent of being able to accommodate changes in activities and requirements during a lifespan of 50 years or more.

1.2   Design and construction methods

There are two basic approaches, each with variations, which a client can adopt for the design and construction of new building work, and an early decision has to be taken on which general method will be most appropriate for the project.

One option is to employ independent consultants for the design and then, at a later stage, a contractor to build the project. This method is used for many projects of all types and sizes undertaken by private clients, and has several advantages. For example, it allows the freedom to choose a briefing and design team most suited to one's specific needs from the large variety of consultant firms. It also allows the freedom to obtain competitive tenders for the construction, based on the same drawings and specifications, although it is possible for the design team to negotiate with a single contractor.

The other option is to employ a single firm for both the design and the construction of the project, a method also referred to as a 'package deal' or a 'turn-key' operation. There are a variety of construction companies offering this type of integrated service. Some supply standard buildings only, some undertake one-off projects, some do both; some specialise in building types, for example, warehouses, factories, offices, hotels, schools or housing; some produce building systems which they use in their projects; some specialise in simple single-storey structures, while others undertake complex and multi-storey projects. These companies employ their own professional staff, either in-house or outside consultants, who develop the brief and design for specific projects. Although it is possible to approach different companies and have each submit a proposal, it can be difficult to compare prices as they will not be based on identical designs and specifications. The client may, furthermore, have to bear the costs of the proposals submitted by the unsuccessful firms. While this method may save time and/or money on certain types of projects, a disadvantage can be the lack of advice from the consultants of one's own choice.

Which of the two basic methods is used will depend largely on the nature of the problem, the type, size and complexity of the proposed project, as well as the time available for its completion. It is ultimately up to the client and his initial advisers to investigate alternatives and make sure that participants, whether independent consultants or design/construct firms, are carefully selected.

1.3   The brief and the briefing process

Once the client has decided to investigate the possibility of altering, extending or converting an existing building, or erecting a new one, the first phase of the proposed project begins. This is the development of the brief through the process of briefing.

A brief is usually a document which can vary considerably in length, content and form depending upon the nature and complexity of the project. It is, amongst other things, a recorded statement of intent and a set of criteria and instructions, including proposals by the design team approved by the client. It is influenced by and derived from the consideration of many factors such as budget, climate, site, legal constraints, user requirements, the way things are used and change through time, and the trade-off between cost and feasibility. It states a set of desired

Fig. 1.1 *Different forms of brief: this may be either one of the four shown or a combination of them (e.g. 1 and 4), and typical organisation of contents.*

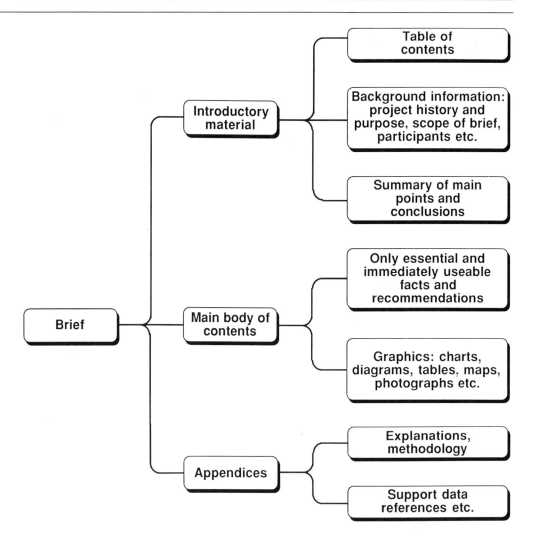

conditions and it is a way of defining, ordering and specifying objectives, requirements and intentions systematically, as well as outlining the methods for achieving them.

Rather than being an end in itself, the brief is a tool that can help those involved to achieve certain desirable ends. It can be used in different ways depending on the problem. For example, a preliminary brief can assist the client to select the right designers and other specialist advisers; a more developed brief (interim or final) may be used as a competition document or a contractual document forming part of a legal agreement between the client and other parties. Although the ultimate goal is usually to provide the specific information and recommendations that are needed and can be used for designing the building, the brief is also used to determine feasibility and may lead to the abandonment of the project.

Starting with a preliminary statement prepared by the client (possibly with professional help), the brief is developed and constantly refined through a process

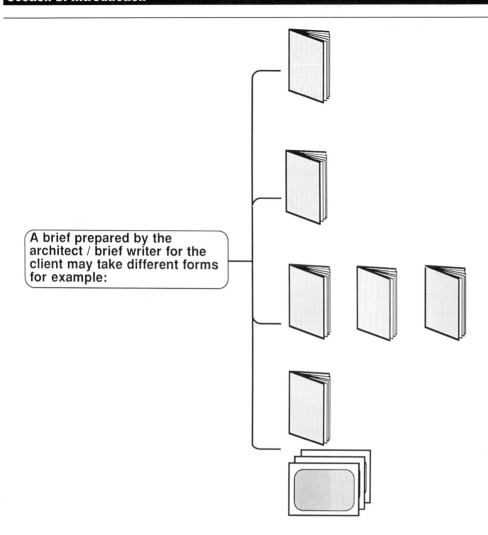

1. *A short preliminary report.*

2. *A comprehensive document covering all aspects of the building design.*

3. *A series of reports relating definable issues or phased accomplishments.*

4. *A special purpose report covering a specific aspect such as energy conservation or site analysis/survey. This may also take the form of an audiovisual presentation.*

A brief prepared by the architect / brief writer for the client may take different forms for example:

of communication, investigation, analysis and evaluation. The process of briefing is, in other words, one of dialogue between all concerned; a process of finding as well as solving problems; of determining and defining objectives, constraints, resources, subjective and objective criteria; of determining and exploring what is appropriate and possible, evaluating proposals and making recommendations. Briefing is often controversial since, while technical requirements can usually be quantified, this is often not possible with other more abstract criteria. It should therefore be a process of debate and a means of decision-making, encouraging participation by, and feedback from, all the participants.

The brief, therefore, changes and grows continuously as the design proceeds. The design solution evolves from the brief and can, in turn, clarify and expand it through early design work which helps to identify problems, objectives and criteria. When it is realised in the completed project, it also has a role in post-construction evaluation. After a certain point in the design process, which will

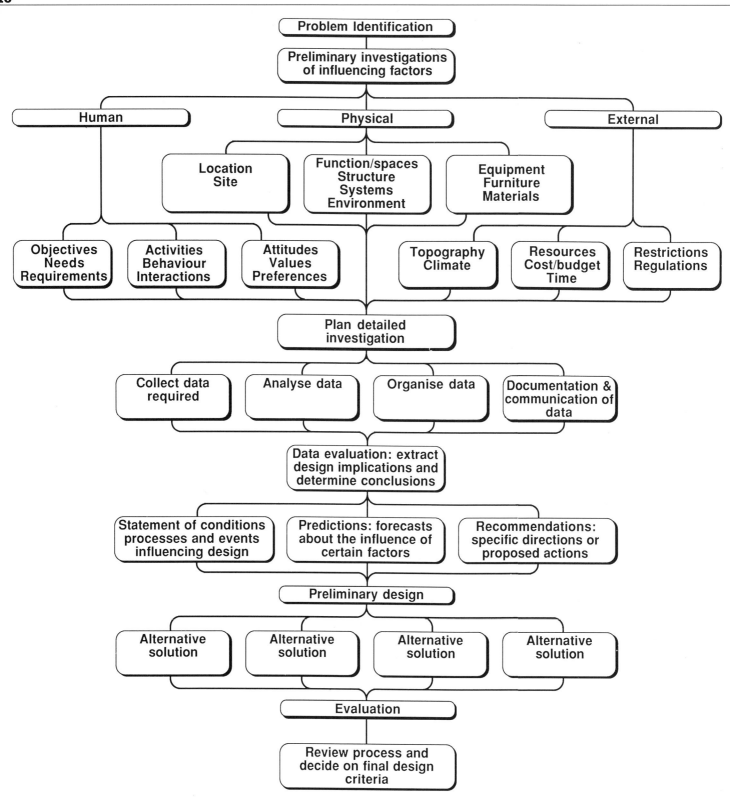

Problem Identification

Preliminary investigations of influencing factors

Human

Physical

External

Location
Site

Function/spaces
Structure
Systems
Environment

Equipment
Furniture
Materials

Objectives
Needs
Requirements

Activities
Behaviour
Interactions

Attitudes
Values
Preferences

Topography
Climate

Resources
Cost/budget
Time

Restrictions
Regulations

Plan detailed
investigation

Collect data
required

Analyse data

Organise data

Documentation &
communication of
data

Data evaluation: extract
design implications and
determine conclusions

Statement of conditions
processes and events
influencing design

Predictions: forecasts
about the influence of
certain factors

Recommendations:
specific directions or
proposed actions

Preliminary design

Alternative
solution

Alternative
solution

Alternative
solution

Alternative
solution

Evaluation

Review process and
decide on final design
criteria

vary from project to project, major changes to the brief can lead to abortive work and have cost implications for the client or the design team.

Although, as has already been stressed, there is no one way of approaching briefing, it always forms the foundation of the design process and constitutes an integral part of this process. For these reasons and because there are usually so many factors and variables involved in the design of even the simplest building, it is important that the brief be objectively, imaginatively and comprehensively developed whatever the method used.

1.4 The main participants

The main groups involved in the process of briefing and design are the client, the users, the professional brief writer and the design team.

The client

The client is the person or organisation initiating and paying for the project. There are many different types of client ranging from private individuals to complex private and public organisations. Not only is the nature of each type different but so also are their needs, objectives, values, priorities, resources and restraints. Some build for their own use; others are providers of space rather than users of the building; yet others act for and on behalf of the actual users; for some, building is a commercial venture, while for others the basic motive may, for example, have to do with welfare, education or culture.

While clients in the public sector are controlled by predetermined rules and procedures affecting organisation, approval, financing and time-scale, private clients have relative freedom. Client responsibilities also tend to differ. In the public sector, the client departments are very often responsible not only for initiating the project, selecting the site, instructing the consultants and monitoring progress, but also for gathering and co-ordinating information from various departments, producing the initial brief and preparing the documents required for outline planning applications, loan sanctions, and so on.

Private clients, on the other hand, often leave some of these responsibilities, for example, the gathering and organisation of basic data, and preparation of an initial (or preliminary) brief, to the architect. Alternatively they may appoint a professional brief writer to assist them. At an early stage the client must determine the extent of his personal involvement which should, at the very least, be sufficient to ensure that responsibilities delegated to others are being adequately discharged.

It is not difficult for individual clients or small organisations to have a simple, ideally single, line of contact between themselves and the other participants. However, the more complex the client body – the greater the number of people, departments and sections involved, and the greater the levels of hierarchy – the more difficult it becomes to determine just who is the client. It follows that in this case it is important for the roles and responsibilities of all those involved, in management, professional and advisory capacities, and for the channels of communication (particularly on a day-to-day basis) to be clearly defined to avoid delays and confusion.

Fig. 1.2 *Although the briefing process can be approached in different ways, the flow chart at left outlines the common activities involved in developing the required information.*

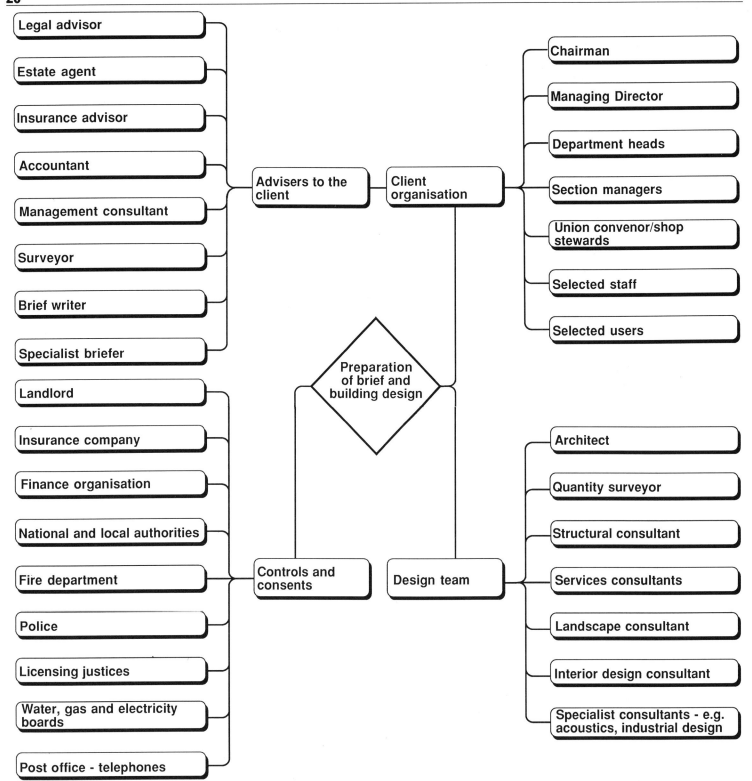

Legal advisor
Estate agent
Insurance advisor
Accountant
Management consultant
Surveyor
Brief writer
Specialist briefer

Advisers to the client

Client organisation

Chairman
Managing Director
Department heads
Section managers
Union convenor/shop stewards
Selected staff
Selected users

Preparation of brief and building design

Landlord
Insurance company
Finance organisation
National and local authorities
Fire department
Police
Licensing justices
Water, gas and electricity boards
Post office - telephones

Controls and consents

Design team

Architect
Quantity surveyor
Structural consultant
Services consultants
Landscape consultant
Interior design consultant
Specialist consultants - e.g. acoustics, industrial design

The users

The users are those who will actually use the building: they may live, work, play or relax in it; they may be permanent inhabitants or employees who use it daily, or members of the general public who visit it regularly or occasionally. Clients and users are very often different bodies: public authorities and speculative developers are examples of clients who, together with their professional consultants, brief and design on behalf of the eventual users. As a result, few users have the opportunity of influencing the original design, and all too often their requirements and likely use of the spaces are based on assumptions.

In many building types there is the problem of different kinds of users. In hospitals, for example, nurses, doctors, patients and visitors are all users. They may have different or even conflicting requirements. The various categories of user must be identified at an early stage as it is important to understand the implications of their requirements, and to be responsive to them. How this is done will depend on circumstances and vary from project to project. One or more of the following methods may be used:

— direct involvement and participation: permanent staff or regular users may be represented or consulted through unions, local organisations and pressure groups. This encourages an active role in the process by helping to define problems and objectives, to generate concepts and evaluate alternatives. In some instances this might be essential, while in others it might hinder the process or be impossible.

— social science and other user studies: a helpful source of data, but care should be taken because such studies may be generalised and in the planning of a building specific requirements are necessary. On the other hand it must also be borne in mind that the very specific data which is often provided in these studies may not necessarily be relevant to any one particular problem. If studies are to be carried out specifically for a project by surveys, interviews, questionnaires or observation, for example, the designers' limitations must be taken into account and collaboration with suitable consultants from the field of human sciences should be considered.

— surveys of similar building types in use to provide feedback on user requirements. Many of the building studies published in architectural journals tend to concentrate on visual aesthetics and technical aspects, lacking sufficient information on actual usage. If private surveys are undertaken, the method of study and appraisal should place emphasis on evidence from various users: on the deficiencies and advantages they find while living, working, playing or relaxing in the building in question.

The professional brief writer

The professional brief writer specialises in helping clients determine and describe their building needs. This person is, generally speaking, qualified not only to carry out analytical, objective, unbiased and creative studies of the clients' and users' needs, but also to understand their implications for design. He may be:

— a member of the client organisation.

Fig. 1.3 *People who may be involved in the briefing and design process. Just who will participate will depend, amongst other things, on the size of the client organisation and on the type and complexity of the project.*

— an architect who provides a briefing service either separately or as part of design services (see also Appendix A.4).
— a professional brief writer, who may or may not be an architect, but who specialises in the process of briefing and the preparation of briefs.
— a briefing specialist who provides a service for a particular building type.

The professional brief writer may only be involved with preparing an initial policy-briefing document or may be retained, with the approval of the architect and other members of the design team, to help develop a detailed brief, and possibly to help evaluate plans and proposals, as the work progresses.

The design team

The design team is made up of the architect together with various other appointed consultants each of whom specialise in one aspect of the design process. The team may include a quantity surveyor, structural, electrical and mechanical engineers, an interior designer, a landscape architect, as well as other specialists from various disciplines, possibly used on a short-term or *ad hoc* basis as dictated by the project. The responsibilities of this group include advising the client and users of the options available to them, assisting with the development of the brief, and carrying out the actual designing and managing activities.

In very large or very complex projects it may be necessary to include an experienced project manager or project controller who would be responsible for the overall co-ordination and monitoring of the total project from inception to completion. This person may be an architect, surveyor or engineer specialising exclusively in this service, and usually also acts as the liaison officer between all the parties involved.

All these consultants are generally in private practices, and although some large consultant firms may include a variety of specialists under one roof they are certain to need outside help on occasion. The same is true of the public sector and large private client organisations that have their own design offices.

1.5 Approvals

Another group of people who, although not directly involved in the briefing and design process, exert an important influence on all phases of the work, are the representatives of the various public authorities responsible for applying the appropriate legislation and regulations. There is a vast amount which governs new building work and involves discussion with and formal application to various public authorities. For example:

— planning applications – for new developments, changes of use and certain extensions – to the appropriate local planning authority. These are usually in two stages: the first is an 'outline' application giving information on the general intention; the second is a 'full' application accompanied by drawings illustrating the scheme in detail.
— application to the local authority responsible for administering the Building Regulations. Detailed drawings, specifications and structural

calculations must be submitted and approval obtained before any construction work begins.

— the local fire authority must inspect and approve premises before issuing a fire certificate; the local health officer and the district surveyor will need to be consulted on requirements for fire precautions, lighting, ventilation and the provision of sanitary conveniences.

— other individuals or organisations may have to be consulted or give their approval: for example, the local gas, electricity, water and telephone authorities; the landlord or lessor; the insurance company; owners of adjoining properties.

It will be evident from this introduction that the statutory implications of embarking on new building work can be daunting to say the least. The exercise of attending to the requirements is a time-consuming and often a frustrating one, usually taken care of by the architect and other members of the design team. However, some applications, such as special licences, have to be attended to by the client himself, possibly with legal help.

Inception and the preliminary brief

The aim of this phase is to prepare a general outline of requirements and to plan future action. The procedure is a sequence of actions, listed below, which, generally speaking, is standard (in basics only) for all projects irrespective of building type. These steps are supplementary to those given under Section 2, 'Inception and initial brief', and should be used in conjunction with them.

The client must take certain action, possibly with professional help, before any real work on the brief commences. The problem must be defined: the questions who? what? why? where? when? and how? must be considered.

1.6 Client to define problem

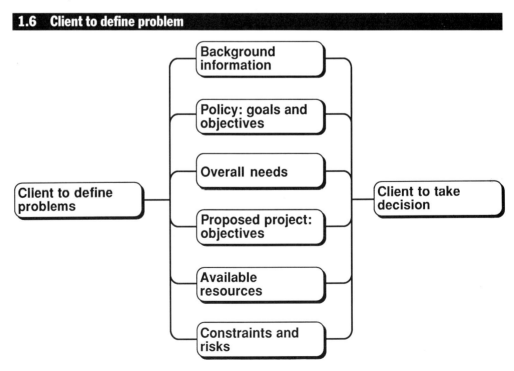

Background information

Describe the client enterprise/body as fully as possible, for example:
—   function or purpose for existence, and activities.
—   philosophy and history.
—   structure and method of operation.
—   characteristics: whether conservative or experimental, formal or informal.
—   existing facilities with information on problems.

Policy: goals and objectives

Determine what the aims and policies are for future growth and change in terms of:
—   overall functions to be fulfilled.
—   size, achievement, performance, organisation.
—   short (2-year), medium (5-year) and long (10-year-plus) term.
Consider:
—   why these objectives are important. What the alternatives are. Who will benefit from the achievement of the objectives.
—   other parties involved (for example, user groups) who may have different or conflicting objectives.
—   what the overriding priorities are.

Overall needs

Estimate present and future overall needs in terms of:
—   number and type of staff and/or users.
—   activities and equipment to be housed.
Estimate need for additional building space over short (2-year), medium (5-year) and long (10-year-plus) term.

Proposed project: objectives

Formulate in general terms (not detail) objectives for, and broad scope of, proposed project: What is required of it? What will it include and exclude? What are the priorities?
Consider:
—   location, site, relationship with other buildings, landscaping.
—   size of proposed building: number of people, type of process and equipment, activities it must accommodate. What floor area is required?
—   special spaces or facilities required and special equipment to be housed.
—   internal environment: ventilation, lighting, heating and services.
—   energy use/conservation.
—   maintenance.
—   lifespan and flexibility: probable changes of use over time.
—   prestige level externally and internally: appearance, height of building/spaces, quality of finishes.
—   timing: How important is completion date? How urgent is starting date? Can project be done in phases?
—   cost implications within a time-frame.

Members of the client body (for example, management, department heads, key staff) should be brought in and encouraged to assist with the various aspects of problem definition and formulation of objectives.

Although it may not be appropriate to set up a briefing and design team at this stage, preliminary general advice may be needed on various aspects such as legal, estate, management and financial which will vary with such factors as the experience of the client and the size and complexity of the proposed project.

At this stage all that it requires are broad guidelines rather than rigid details; there must be flexibility for continual development and change – for additions, omissions and revisions.

To generate and develop ideas, and establish priorities, techniques such as brain storming may be useful. See Appendix A.5 for a summary of these and references to useful sources of more detailed information.

Fig. 1.4 *Defining and ranking objectives.*

1 = objective in row is preferred to objective in column

0 = objective in column is preferred to objective in row

It is impossible to start the process of briefing and design without first defining objectives which are, because of the nature of the problem, difficult to separate from the ways of achieving them. One way of exploring and clarifying objectives is to construct an objective 'tree'. Start by listing the known objectives. For example, when considering the design of fire protection for a building the broad goals might be to:
— reduce likelihood of death or injury to occupants and users.
— protect the building fabric.
— protect the contents.

Each of these can be expanded into sub-objectives that can be further sub-divided:

The first basic objective, to reduce likelihood of death and injury, can be analysed in the same way. The objective 'tree' itself does not provide any answers and these are most likely to come as a result of working through the process itself: as a result of asking oneself the questions what? why? how? The exercise should provide a starting-point for discussion that will help to identify which objectives really are essential, which are compatible with each other, and how each relates to the resources available.

Once objectives are identified a matrix can be used to help determine objectives. The value of this method becomes more apparent when there is a large list of objectives to consider making it more difficult to rank them intuitively. One disadvantage is that comparison by pairs can result in illogical responses, for example, choosing B over A, A over C and then C over B. If such a matrix is filled in by a number of people the results should be randomly checked for such responses to ensure that they are valid.

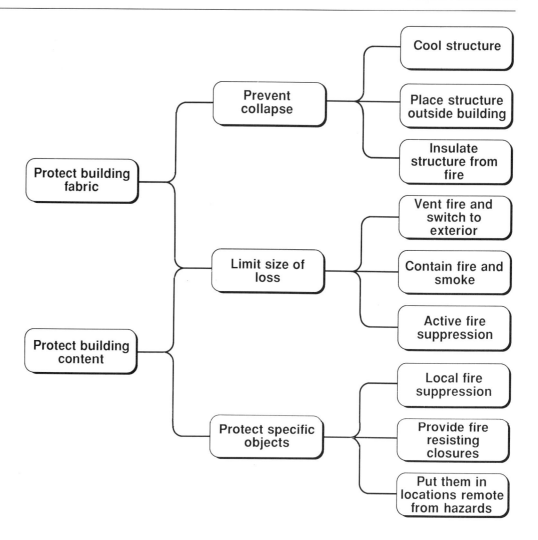

Objective	A	B	C	D	E	Row totals	Ranking
A		0	0	0	1	1	4
B	1		1	0	1	3	2
C	1	0		0	1	2	3
D	1	1	1		1	4	1
E	0	0	0	0		0	5

Available resources

Estimate your own and all other available present and future resources, for example:

— own finance, manpower, time, building space and land.
— access to other finance: share issue, grants and loans.
— availability of materials, manpower, energy and land.

Constraints and risks

Determine all possible constraints:

— shortage of resources, for example, finance and time, and/or cost of capital needed.
— site.
— legal and consents: special licence required, planning consent.
— tax implications in terms of time-scale.

Consider various ways of reconciling need and objectives with available resources without undue risk, for example:

— cash flow and commitment of resources.
— risk assessment, spread and sharing.

1.7   Decision

In terms of the foregoing consider reasons for and against building:

— is there really a need or demand for the type of facility under review?
— relate potential need/demand and stated objectives to resources, constraints and risks: What does one wish to accomplish? Will it be possible to achieve this?

Consider which of the following will be most appropriate:

— decrease demand or need for building space.
— rent space.
— buy building suited to needs.
— buy and convert building.
— expand or adapt present accommodation.
— build new building.

This is a preliminary decision only: it is a decision to proceed to the next stage, that is to invest time and a predetermined sum of money to start the formal process of briefing and design in order to investigate in detail the feasibility of the proposed project.

A decision to go ahead may be the correct one at this stage. The briefing and design process extends over a period of time, however, and as new information becomes available at a later stage it will be necessary to review the decision.

1.8 Initial procedures by client

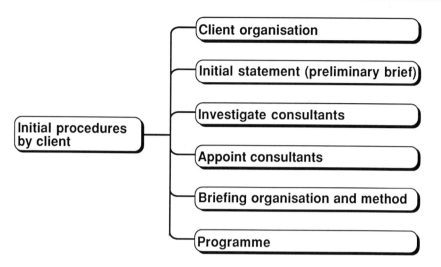

Initial procedures by client
- Client organisation
- Initial statement (preliminary brief)
- Investigate consultants
- Appoint consultants
- Briefing organisation and method
- Programme

Client organisation

Set up organisation for decision-making and for management of the project from the client side.

Consider the following:

— committee or working party.

— departmental representatives.

— liaison with briefing and design team particularly on a day-to-day basis.

Determine roles and responsibilities of all concerned including who will be responsible for initial statement:

— is there sufficient expertise within the client organisation to do the required work?

— if not, consider appointing a professional brief writer or approaching specialists appropriate to this task.

Initial statement (preliminary brief)

This statement should be based on information and ideas used to arrive at the decision to proceed. It may be prepared by the client, someone within the client organisation or a professional brief writer.

Steps listed under 1.9 can be used as a checklist for the kind of information that should be included.

Prepare a written preliminary document: a statement of aims and requirements including all available relevant information. Describe:

— the nature of the client body and the implications of that fact.

— why a building is needed.

— what objectives should be met by the proposed building, setting out priorities.

Investigate consultants

Determine what consultants will be required at this stage and whether they should be appointed for developing the brief only or for briefing and design:

— professional brief writer and/or briefing specialist.
— architect.
— surveyor: for obtaining accurate site information or when adapting/converting existing building.
— quantity surveyor: for cost estimates.
— structural, mechanical and electrical engineers.
— other specialists: landscape architect, interior designer.

Investigate suitable firms and ascertain position with regard to services provided, fees, contracts etc. Consider, amongst other things:

— experience of architects and other consultants in dealing with similar building types/projects.
— personalities: close working relationship and confidence between all concerned is important.

For summarised guidance on services offered, fees charged etc. by the main groups of consultants see Appendix A.4.

The type and size of project, as well as, amongst other things, the aesthetic qualities envisaged will influence the choice of architect and the decision on what other consultants/specialists are required.

Appoint consultants

Approach selected firms and discuss terms. Appoint the following:

— architect: to prepare brief only; or for complete project; or something in between.
— other consultants required now; further appointments may have to be made at a later stage.

Consult architect for his recommendations regarding the most suitable consultants.

Formal agreement should include definitions of limits of responsibility, precise scope of services to be provided, time implications, details of fees and expenses etc. Standard forms may be used; exchange of letters may be adequate.

Briefing organisation and method

Establish formal organisation for briefing and design process: committee, steering group etc. Identify likely participants and define:

— relationship to client organisation.
— a single client instruction route. This is particularly important if the client is a public authority or a government department, or in the case of a joint use project with more than one client.
— responsibilities and procedures, for example, administration and control.
— role to be played in process by users and/or user organisations.

Decide on briefing methods:

— communication: regular meetings, circulation of documents etc.
— documentation, for example, recording of data and decisions for easy retrieval and reference.
— techniques: surveys, use of computer etc.

An outline of some briefing methods and techniques is given in Appendix A.5; for more detailed information see Appendix A.1.a: Jones[1], Palmer[2], Preiser[3] and Sanoff[4].

Use Section 2 as a checklist of steps to be taken/tasks to be done. A simple linear sequence will not, however, be suitable for drawing up a programme since there is bound to be overlapping. Techniques are available to help in the preparation of charts that relate overlapping steps to time. See Fig. 1.5.

A quantity surveyor and an accountant will be best suited to give advice on building economics and financial implications. For outline information see Appendix A.4.

Programme

Identify and schedule briefing and design work:
—   list tasks to be done and decisions to be made.
—   assign responsibilities: who will be involved with each task and when.
—   estimate financial and other resources needed.
Determine realistic timetable. Consider:
—   key target dates set by external circumstances: expiry of lease on existing premises etc.
—   dates for building commencement and completion.
—   effect of seasons on building operations.
—   scope of project and quality of work required.
—   availability of manpower.

Fig. 1.5 *A. A simple bar chart showing estimated duration of sequential steps or activities in relation to a time scale. Dependencies between the activities are not indicated in such a chart. This means that should one activity be delayed it is not immediately apparent how this will affect subsequent events. B. A critical path method (CPM) chart in which interconnecting arrows form a network diagram with the time of each activity shown below each arrow (in curved brackets). This is a sophisticated method used for charting time overlaps and activity interdependencies amongst other things, and from which the critical path – the sequence of interdependent activities which establishes the shortest possible time in which a project can be completed – is determined.*

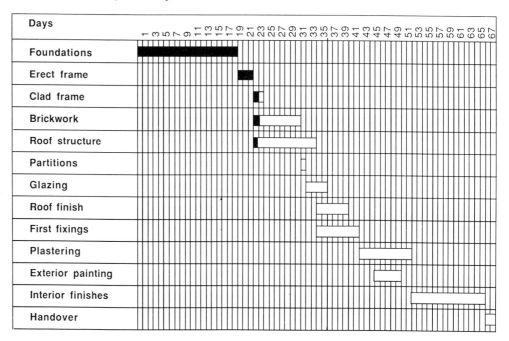

A.

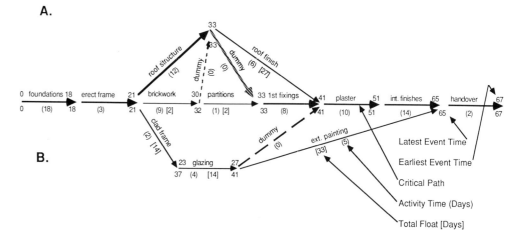

B.

— cash flow over time.
— financial implications of timing, for example, income on investment versus interest paid on loan.

1.9 General data and objectives

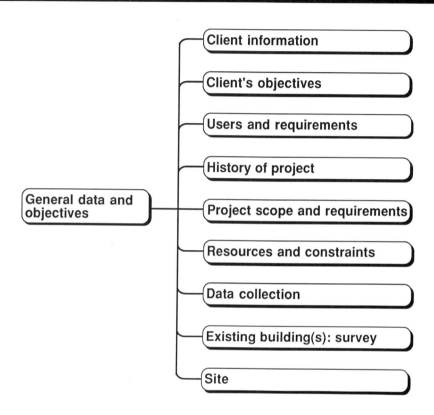

Although addressed to the architect the following should be used by the client, and whoever assists him, as a guideline to the information required in the 'Initial statement' (see p.28). Read together with 2.6.

Client information

Evaluate preliminary client statement. Check that all information on the nature and character of the client enterprise/body is available:
— what they do, how they do it: public authority, joint venture, private concern or other.
— whom they employ or collaborate with.
— involvement with outside services.
— corporate priorities and the likelihood of change.

Client's objectives

Ensure that all information regarding the client's overriding objectives and priorities – both short and long term – is available:

— financial return required or service to the community (social, cultural, educational).
— image to be projected.
— planned or predicted growth and likelihood of change.

Users and requirements

Establish who the potential users are if not the client. If possible take steps to contact the different kinds of users. Decide how user requirements are to be communicated/determined, for example:

— direct involvement/consultation: through union or elected representatives.
— and/or through questionnaire/survey.
— and/or through building studies.

History of project

Check whether any work has previously been undertaken:

— feasibility or other.
— have any other consultants been involved? Has their work been paid for?
— have any decisions already been made?
— has data already been collected?

Project scope and requirements

Determine the scope, limitations and basic requirements of the proposed project:

— demand for the type of facility envisaged.
— proposed size; future expansion; phasing? If maximum predicted space is built immediately can present surplus be sub-let?
— degree of flexibility/adaptability required, i.e. the likely use of the building over a period of time.
— character envisaged.
— interface with outside world, for example, free or controlled access.
— requirements for space and equipment; relationships between component parts, individuals etc; standards for accommodation – environmental, finishes etc.
— other criteria, for example, energy conservation.

Method(s) used will vary with circumstances and building type. For a broad description of survey methods see Appendix A.5.

It may be necessary to contact any other architect involved in accordance with RIBA code of conduct.
If possible/relevant go through client records and documents for information directly related to proposed project. Avoid duplicating work already done, for example, data collection.

Who decides what will depend upon circumstances. The architect and/or professional brief writer must, however, ensure that the client and users are aware of the available options, and that the necessary decisions are made and understood by all.
See Appendix A.1.a: Alexander[5] which is a useful tool for all involved in the briefing and design process: a variety of options at various levels/scales are listed and described.

Resources and constraints

Ensure that all necessary information on available resources and possible constraints is either included in the initial statement or, alternatively, obtained from the client. Consider particularly:

— budget (cost limit): what is included in the cost of building, equipment and furniture, landscaping, consultants' fees?

— whether the effects of inflation have been taken into account.

— recommended and mandatory standards, statutory requirements, regulations and restrictions affecting the project. Draw up a list for reference purposes.

— other resources that can be used (expertise, manpower) and imposed constraints (cash flow, time limits).

— how the resources and constraints relate to the requirements and objectives.

For detailed information on the building regulations in the UK see Appendix A.1.a: Elder[6a]; Speaight[7] is a useful reference covering the law of property and land and building regulations amongst other things.

Data collection

Organise and analyse data presently available. Consider:

— relevance, relationships, priorities.

— what information still needs to be obtained and/or confirmed. For what purpose?

— the form in which it is required, by when it will be needed and who will carry out the various tasks. How will this affect the programme?

— the primary information sources for the different kinds of data needed; client, user groups, publications.

Gather data in relation to stated needs/objectives and in time to be useful; confine initial surveys (user requirements, site) to bare essentials, and to data that are readily available and immediately useful. Balance the penalty of insufficient information against the cost of obtaining it. Store data in a flexible way so that new information can be added readily.

Different techniques may be needed for obtaining different types of data: for summaries of the main methods see Appendix A.5.

Existing building(s): survey

Where applicable, survey/appraise existing building(s): premises presently occupied to be altered/extended or new premises to be converted.

— measure up and prepare survey drawings.

— investigate construction, materials, elements, finishes, services.

— prepare report on all defects including cause and recommended method of correction.

In premises presently occupied, how is client accommodated now? This is useful as basis for comparison even when new building is being planned. Determine:

— how the building has been used through the period of occupation.

— the deficiencies and advantages in terms of the various users' needs.

— running costs, for example, maintenance, operation and changes.

Specific guidance on finding new premises is not given here. Specialist help may be required for the survey and report: to open up and examine foundations and structure; to trace services; to investigate rot, woodworm.

For outline of approach to evaluation of existing buildings see Appendix A.5.

The same basic technique is followed for both site selection and site survey/analysis. Appendix A.2 sets out the requirements in broad outline.

The survey and analysis is a very important part of the brief investigation and development. Data gathering can, however, be expensive and time-consuming and the survey must be well planned. It is generally advisable to employ the services of a qualified surveyor.

Site

Where applicable, investigate site. If client owns specific site:

— visit and inspect.

— check if survey is available; if not, arrange for survey to be prepared.

If site is not fixed:

— investigate alternatives; determine appropriateness for proposed development.

— will owner sell? Is sale price reasonable: how does it compare with valuation by local authority? Are there any legal problems?

— make proposal based on analysis of potential sites.

SECTION TWO
LIBRARIES

Introduction

2.1 General

Libraries are places where books are housed for use either by the general public or by some specific group of people. While the main function of libraries throughout history – as resource centres for information and ideas – has remained unaltered, in recent years these institutions have undergone a phase of rapid development and change that has extended their scope and identity. Not only has the range of communication formats multiplied – in addition to books, periodicals, newspapers and maps libraries now stock audio discs and tapes, information stored on microforms and, in some cases, even ciné films and video cassettes – but so also has the variety of services offered. Some public libraries are fast becoming community centres while the libraries in some education institutions are developing into workshops for creative self-education. As a result of these changes the library today may be called a 'multi-media centre', 'material resources centre', 'learning resources centre' or something similar describing its wider function and purpose.

The ever-changing and advancing technologies of communications and computing have influenced, and will continue to influence, library methods. Some go so far as to say that with this rapid growth in electronics technology, libraries will be unnecessary in the future: information will be stored in central computers and retrieved through terminals located in homes, classrooms or offices. Whether this will become a reality remains to be seen. What is certain, however, is that computer-based acquisition, stock-control, cataloguing and issue control systems are spreading rapidly; and that the pattern of research and the functioning of specialised and research libraries in particular are being affected by, for example, electronic information retrieval and easily produced copies, as well as inter-library lending.

The general consensus of opinion amongst librarians is that it will continue to be the task of the library to acquire, house and process information in whatever form it may be produced in years to come. Books will continue to form the bulk of library stock for the immediate future and will be supplemented to a greater or lesser degree – depending on the type and function of the library – by records, cassettes, tapes, films, microforms and all the apparatus required for these media.

Not enough is known about the continuing changes in the technology of communication to predict exactly how they will influence the library building of the future. The computer, as well as audio-visual and other developments, will without doubt play an increasingly important role and almost certainly make the library very different. It is, therefore, essential to ensure that library buildings are sufficiently flexible to accommodate future developments; to plan them in such a way that almost any part can be used for a diversity of likely functions. This implies, amongst other things, a building with suitable environmental conditions throughout, possibly with a structure that is strong enough to carry heavy loads (of, for example, concentrated bookstacks) anywhere, with services and other fixed elements grouped so as to free the largest area on each floor for changing uses, and with a ceiling height that will be appropriate for a variety of functions.

The relatively recent awareness of older buildings as a resource to be usefully conserved has led to the search for ways of bringing many of them back into active use. As a result a number of effective libraries (as well as a number that are unsuitable for their purpose) now exist in a wide range of converted buildings including houses, palaces, market halls and warehouses. This trend is likely to continue, particularly in the case of old buildings occupying key urban sites. The challenge is not only to select suitable buildings, but also to provide functional and flexible libraries with the required atmosphere within the existing shells.

2.2 Types of client

The client is generally a corporate body, but if a principal librarian has been appointed, he is usually empowered to act as the client on all but cost and major policy decisions. The powers, duties and intentions of library authorities may vary considerably from country to country. Clients are listed below according to type of library.

National
Controlled by boards of trustees or governors. Major projects are subject to approval by appropriate government ministry/department.

Public
Provision is usually in the hands of local government authorities. In the UK two authorities are involved: municipal (borough and urban district) and county serving larger regions which may include several towns and less densely populated rural areas. Funds are normally obtained through a loan sanction granted by the Ministry of Housing and local government after approval of the scheme by the Department of Education and Science.

University and college

The client will usually be a library planning committee or board of trustees and may be represented by the principal librarian and a library building consultant. In the UK university libraries are normally financed by central government funds administered by The University Grants Committee, while funds for college libraries are generally provided by the local education authority.

Schools

In the case of state schools funds are normally provided, subject to ministerial approval, by the local education authority. In private schools libraries may be paid for by private funds and donations. School libraries in all but the largest schools will generally be the charge of a member of the teaching staff.

2.3   Types of library

Generally, libraries fall into one of the following broad categories, but it must be emphasised that there can be a great deal of variation within each category.

National

The primary function of a national library is to collect all nationally published material plus a wide selection of representative foreign publications and to provide facilities for advanced research students. Sometimes national archives are accommodated.

These libraries are regarded as the great warehouses of the national system and, as they generally strive to achieve comprehensiveness, their stocks are usually phenomenally large.

Public

This category includes central (either municipal or county/state) libraries as well as the branch libraries which may be attached to them. They provide a public service and must, therefore, be easily accessible. They may be grouped with, or form part of, a shopping, community, cultural or educational centre and do sometimes provide auxiliary facilities – for example, meeting room, lecture hall, small theatre and/or cinema, restaurant or coffee bar, bookshop – within the library building.

According to the International Federation of Library Associations a public library system (central and branch libraries) should preferably have a population base of at least 150,000. It is only in this situation that it becomes economically possible to provide a comprehensive range of both materials and specialised services.

Central

These complex organisations usually house:

a) The administrative and distribution headquarters for a system of libraries serving a specific area. A population of 50,000 is normally regarded as the minimum for an administrative unit.

b) The 'stack': the accumulation of books which, while not in regular demand, must be held for readers in any part of the area.

c) The specialist services – reference and information, technical, commercial, local history – which are too expensive (in terms of both staff and bookstock) to be duplicated at each branch. A mobile library service may also be provided.

d) The general services provided for those who live in the central area or use it for their shopping needs – mainly lending services but additional functions (lectures, readings, film shows, exhibitions) are often arranged.

Because of the variety of services provided these libraries tend to be sectionalised more than other types so that there are separate departments for adult lending, children, reference and music.

Branch

This provides a lending service (books, records, tapes) and minor reference and study facilities to the local community. What is included depends largely on the character and specific needs of the community. When a demand is chiefly localised a special service is sometimes offered at a branch rather than at the central library: for example, technical stock may be best sited in an area common to industry and the local technical college.

In large systems, some branch libraries may act as parent libraries to the smaller branches in the surrounding area.

Educational

This is a library that forms part of a primary, secondary or further education authority.

University (including polytechnic)

Although the main function is to store information and make it easily and readily available to students, faculty and research workers, the university library is increasingly being regarded as an active participant in teaching and learning programmes.

Collections – which contain a higher than normal proportion of periodicals – are most often housed centrally; they are, however, sometimes partly or largely decentralised in the form of a series of faculty or departmental libraries.

A large proportion of the library stock is usually open for readers to search and is combined with seating/study places for up to 25 or 30 per cent of the student population.

University libraries have traditionally been planned with considerable allowance for expansion. In the UK, however, this trend has been virtually halted as these institutions are now required to be limited in size; beyond a predetermined point stock must be reduced at a rate approaching that of acquisition.

College

Although the function of the college library is similar to that of a university library the scale is smaller as there are fewer students to serve and a more limited range of subjects to cover. There is a growing tendency to provide workshops and laboratories where both staff and students may prepare, process and present audio-visual material.

School

These may vary quite considerably in size and complexity from the small simple libraries in primary schools to those in secondary schools which are more like college libraries.

With the shift in emphasis in many schools from teaching to individual learning, the role of the library has changed accordingly. It has become the focal point of the school, both in terms of function and layout, housing all the resources of modern education. It is commonly called the learning materials resources centre.

Memorial

This can be a library of any type set up to commemorate a distinguished person, or a collection of all material – letters, manuscripts, books – relating to a famous (usually literary) figure. Emphasis is on the preservation of material.

Special

Some libraries do not fall in any of the above categories but have collections limited in range (subject or material) with great depth of coverage. They may vary greatly in size: some, for instance libraries for the blind, may be quite large, but they tend, generally speaking, to be smaller than central public or university libraries and seldom occupy separate buildings. The main types are:

a)   Special user, for example, blind readers, prisoners, hospital patients.

b)   Special material, for example, gramophone records, slides, films, maps, music, periodicals, cuttings, drawings, paintings, archives.

c)   Special subject, for example, attached to a professional institution, learned society, private industrial or commercial organisation or government department.

There is, in most cases, a range of alternative methods used to improve the facilities of the library service in question:

a)   By designing and constructing a new library either independently on its own site or as part of another building (for example, in a school or polytechnic) or complex of buildings (for example, as part of a community centre). The building may provide a new service for the community in which it is located or replace an existing facility. It may, in some cases, be a dual purpose library functioning, for example, both as a school library and as a public branch library.

b)   By altering, extending and/or modernising existing premises which may be either independent or part of a shared building.

c)   By converting an existing premises (house, warehouse) for library use.

2.4   Scope of guide

The three major functional elements – reading, book storage and staff working areas – and the normal cycle of uses they house – location, retrieval and communication of information as well as its return to storage – are more or less common to all types of libraries. The relative importance of the elements and functions, and the spatial and environmental emphases required, will depend largely upon the type of material housed as well as on how it is processed and used. It is generally these differences that will play the major role in determining the design of a library rather than a simple distinction between types. Thus, although the emphasis of this *Guide* is on the larger library (public or university), much of the information given will be appropriate for any library building.

Inception and initial brief

The object of this phase is to establish enough information about the client's and users' overall requirements to allow the feasibility of the project to be assessed and to set the broad framework within which the design team is to work. The standard sequence of actions, starting with problem definition (1.6), should be followed initially. The steps described in 2.5 and 2.6 are supplementary and pertain specifically to libraries.

See Appendix A.1.a: 'Plan of Work', Stage A in *Architect's Job Book*.

2.5   Initial procedures by client

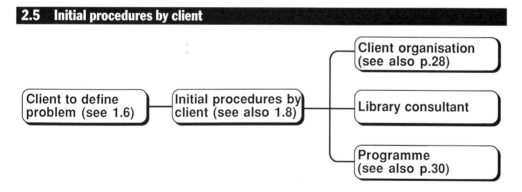

Client organisation

As the client is usually a corporate body with a complex organisational and administrative network the client must define (and the architect verify):

—   what the functions are (in terms of the proposed project) of the various departments, committees and officers who will inevitably be involved.

—   what the responsibilities are of all concerned, for example, the authority's own architect, the consultant architect, the principal librarian, if already appointed.

—   who exactly the client is; who will be taking decisions, giving approvals and instructions.

—   how the liaison between client body and outside consultants will function.

This type of consultant, although rarely used in the UK, is almost always used in the USA and some other countries. Help is given not only with the formulation of the brief but also with evaluating plans and proposals. Advice may be obtained from the local library association (see Appendix A.1.e).

Library consultant

The client to decide whether a library building consultant is to be used. If so, ascertain position with regard to services provided, responsibilities, fees etc. Investigate suitable consultants: check which libraries they have worked on. Ensure that the selected person is appointed as early as possible.

Programme

Ascertain whether time-span for project will be determined or influenced by central government (or other) procedures controlling expenditure.

While Section 2 provides specific information and guidance for the design of libraries, Section 1 offers guidance on the initial procedure basic to all design projects and should be referred to when considering general data and objectives.

2.6   General data and objectives

See 2.3. Note: community use of public libraries is often extended by providing facilities for the activities of local clubs and societies. These may be social, cultural or educational in nature. A library generally provides for some or all of the following activities by users:
– browsing
– reading, viewing and listening
– independent study
– finding of information
– sharing of group experiences
– social contact with other users and with library staff.

Client's objectives and priorities

The client (or principal librarian) to define the type of library required, the role it is intended to play in the life of the community or of the parent body and the relative importance of the main services to be provided, for example:
—   central, branch, departmental, specialist, research or other.
—   dual purpose, such as community library and secondary school library.
—   function as community centre or as part of a larger centre.
—   if part of an institution, provide background information and relationship to other departments/sections.
—   other general objectives both immediate and long term, such as degree of flexibility required.

Information may be obtained from local authority and other local organisations such as the Chamber of Commerce.
The emphasis placed on various objectives of the service – and the means of achieving them – will be different in each community/institution, and will change with the passage of time.

Type of community/institution

Establish what type of community is to be served:
—   rural and/or urban.
—   special characteristics, for example, industrial area containing technical colleges.
—   cultural patterns.
—   local clubs and societies.
—   plans and/or forecasts for future residential, industrial, commercial and educational developments in area.

Population structure

Ascertain present and projected size of population in area or institution. Also the characteristics of the population which have an influence on cultural habits:

— numbers in different age groups: young children, adolescents, retired people.

— population types: students, physically disabled etc.

— for educational institutions: enrolment data and staff size; also projected growth.

If a survey or study is to be carried out decide how institution will be responsible for the work.

See census statistics and local planning department for population figures and details both present and projected. Population figures are often used as a basis for determining bookstock, staff, opening hours and size/type of premises. The IFLA recommends that a population of 3,000 is the minimum required for a library unit; communities smaller than this would need a special service such as a mobile library.

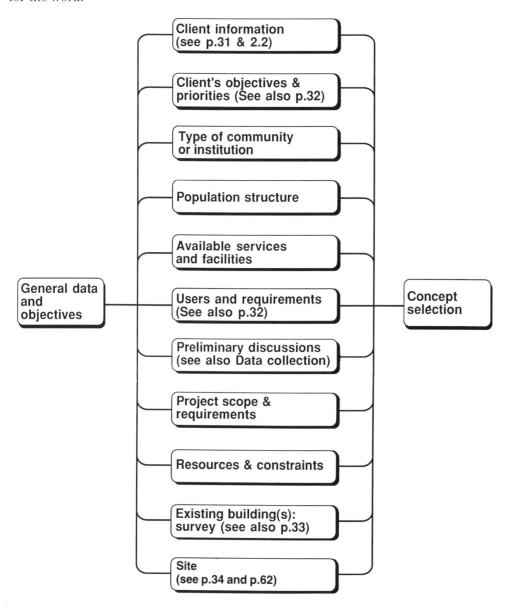

- **General data and objectives**
  - Client information (see p.31 & 2.2)
  - Client's objectives & priorities (See also p.32)
  - Type of community or institution
  - Population structure
  - Available services and facilities
  - Users and requirements (See also p.32)
  - Preliminary discussions (see also Data collection)
  - Project scope & requirements
  - Resources & constraints
  - Existing building(s): survey (see also p.33)
  - Site (see p.34 and p.62)
- **Concept selection**

Provision of facilities for activities of local clubs and societies and for certain adult education activities may be justified so long as unnecessary duplication is avoided.

Available services and facilities

Identify and investigate other local factors that will influence the proposed facility. For example:

— existing and planned libraries and other cultural/educational facilities in or near the area to be served: location, type and (for proposed future developments) timing.

— available transport: public and private.

If a survey or study is to be carried out decide how this will be done and who will be responsible for the work.

For a summary of briefing methods, including questionnaires, surveys, etc, and for an outline of approach to evaluation of existing buildings see Appendix A.5. Direct representation may be most easily achieved at an educational institution (university or college) where user groups (academic staff, students, research workers) are easily identifiable and relatively organised.

Users and requirements

Consider the different types of users – staff and general public or students – and how the requirements of the various groups involved are to be determined:

— direct representation on the briefing and/or planning committee: delegates via staff and student unions/organisations, or local clubs/societies.

— and/or through questionnaire or local survey. If this method is to be used, ascertain who will undertake the work to formulate, distribute and analyse a questionnaire.

— and/or appraisal of similar types of existing library buildings with particular reference to users' comments.

Preliminary discussions

Once objectives have been defined and basic data gathered, arrange meeting of all concerned with briefing process to:

— determine what further exploration should be undertaken.

— establish what specific services and facilities should be provided.

See 2.8. Emphasis on services and activities will depend largely on the general function of the library: provision of suitable study areas and their location in relation to bookstock will be a priority in university and research libraries but not necessarily so in a public library.
As a more detailed guide to the types of services and activities generally accommodated in different kinds of libraries see Appendix A.1.b: Thompson[2], Ellsworth[3,4] and DES[5].

Project scope and requirements

The client/librarian/briefing committee to define the general scope of services, activities and facilities to be included; also, the degree of emphasis to be placed on each of them and the broad level of provision envisaged:

— services for and activities conducted by the public and users of the library, for example, lending department(s), reference, reading/study, information.

— user facilities: photocopying, microform and video cassette viewing, audio reproduction, typing rooms.

— non-library (or associated) activities for adults and children: meetings, readings, lectures, musical recitals, art (and other) exhibitions, refreshment facilities, bookshop.

— mobile library service.

Resources and constraints

Discuss and/or determine:

— availability of funds to meet capital, operational and maintenance costs.

— possible income to be derived from letting expansion space, or hiring facilities (lecture hall, exhibition areas) to outside bodies.

— limits of expenditure and the basis for computing costs.

— what, if any, outline approval/consents must be obtained and, if so, who will be responsible for doing this; also, what specific statutory requirements are applicable. Consult relevant bodies (Department of Education and Science; University Grants Committee; local authority, etc.).

— what, if any, official standards are to be applied – in terms of basic library service, stock and/or size of building.

The cost of a library service is largely determined by the annual operating expenses (staff salaries, purchase of stock and the cost of lighting, heating, cleaning and maintenance) which may be as much as 25 to 50 per cent of the capital cost of the building (see Appendix A.1.b: Brawne[7]).

The latest information on trends, recent development and standard can be obtained from the local Library Association and the library advisers at the DES (see Appendix A.1.e). For information on standards see Appendix A.1.b: Thompson[2], *Standards for Public Libraries*[1] and Withers[6].

Existing building(s): survey

If project is conversion of (or addition to) an existing building arrange for survey. Consider in particular:

— suitability of building for conversion to a library in terms of structure, function, flexibility and aesthetic appeal.

— the potential for future extension either vertically or horizontally.

— whether it will be reasonably easy and not too expensive to modernise/ extend the services: power supply, heating and cooling, fire protection, lighting etc.

In the case of an existing library, consider:

— number of adults and children visiting the library daily.

— how well the existing facilities are used.

— what facilities/services need to be expanded or added.

— which existing facilities/services could be reduced, combined with others or eliminated.

Determine:

— whether building is listed or in a scheduled area.

— whether it will be possible to obtain consent to change the use and/or alter the building.

See also Appendix A.5. In the UK consent for altering use involves obtaining planning permission from the local planning authority. Application is usually made in two stages. The first, or outline, application should be made as early as possible.

2.7 Concept selection

See Fig. 2.1 for a broad outline of various fundamental ways in which libraries may be arranged.

Initial rough estimate of floor area required may be based on 0.09 m² per person for up to 10,000 population served; allow 0.05m² per person for 10,000-100,000 population served. Floor area may be approximately divided as follows: stack 30-40 per cent; seating 20-30 per cent; staff work and storage 15-20 per cent; circulation, lavatories and services 15-20 per cent; ancillary facilities up to 10 per cent.

The development of the brief is usually carried out in progressive steps, in an increasing degree of detail. It is useful if this process is integrated simultaneously with the development of the building design so that there is interaction with the early design work. This will not only help to identify problems but will also lead to the testing of initial thoughts and the questioning of any preconceived ideas.

Consider the various *basic* strategic design concepts which are possible. Keep in mind in particular:

— stated objectives and overriding priorities.
— constraints (site, cost).
— method of book storage (open or closed access) and system of control.
— circulation/communication: between readers and staff and readers and books.
— flexibility required and allowance for growth.
— number of staff available.
— energy consumption/conservation.
— natural versus artificial lighting.

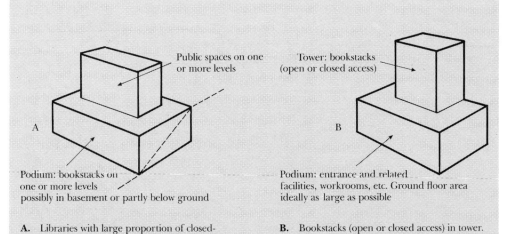

Public spaces on one or more levels

Tower: bookstacks (open or closed access)

A

B

Podium: bookstacks on one or more levels possibly in basement or partly below ground

Podium: entrance and related facilities, workrooms, etc. Ground floor area ideally as large as possible

A. Libraries with large proportion of closed-access bookstacks. Advantages: bookstacks can have lower ceilings, less expensive finishes and fitting and compact storage. Disadvantages: inflexible (i.e. areas not interchangeable); restricted freedom of users; may be difficult to extend

B. Bookstacks (open or closed access) in tower. If closed access advantages and disadvantages as for A. In both cases an additional disadvantage is need to provide staff on each level

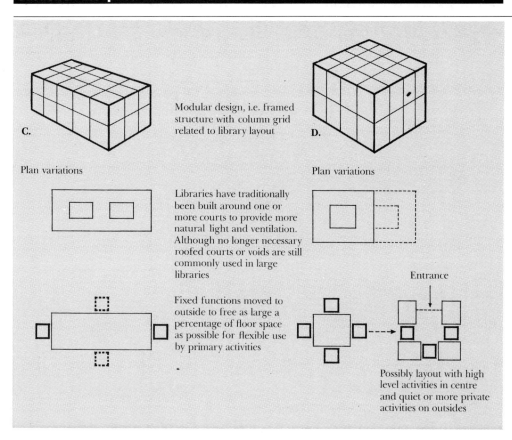

Fig. 2.1 *Some basic design concepts – there are obviously further alternatives, for example an irregular shape may be desirable because of site or some other reason.*

C. Modular design, i.e. framed structure with column grid related to library layout

D.

Plan variations

Plan variations

Libraries have traditionally been built around one or more courts to provide more natural light and ventilation. Although no longer necessary roofed courts or voids are still commonly used in large libraries

Fixed functions moved to outside to free as large a percentage of floor space as possible for flexible use by primary activities

Entrance

Possibly layout with high level activities in centre and quiet or more private activities on outsides

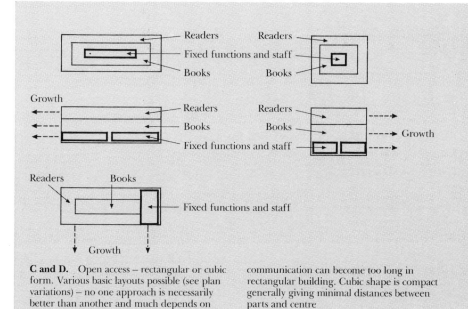

Readers

Readers

Fixed functions and staff

Books

Books

Growth

Readers

Readers

Books

Books

Growth

Fixed functions and staff

Readers   Books

Fixed functions and staff

Growth

C and D. Open access – rectangular or cubic form. Various basic layouts possible (see plan variations) – no one approach is necessarily better than another and much depends on individual circumstances. Lines of communication can become too long in rectangular building. Cubic shape is compact generally giving minimal distances between parts and centre

2.8   Services to be accommodated

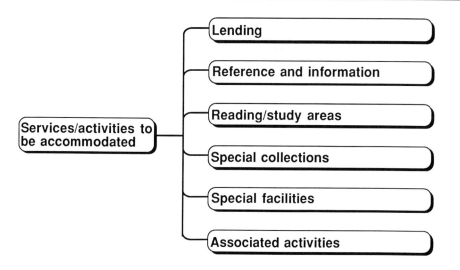

Lending

Establish what services are to be provided and, in each case, for how many users at one time:

See 2.24.1.
Certain decisions (for example, whether to separate or combine adults and children) may be dependent on staff and control considerations. See 2.10.

—   separate departments for adults and children.

—   special zones or sections, for example, for young adults/adolescents.

—   specialised departments: music, art etc.

Determine the types and approximate quantities of material to be accommodated (books, records, tapes, pictures) and whether in separate spaces or zones.

Reference and information

Establish what services are to be provided and, in each case, for how many users at one time:

See 2.24.1.
The increasing use of telecommunication systems and networks (computers with data banks, teleprinters, facsimile transmitters etc.) is likely to influence reference departments, for example, increased space requirements for hardware. Specialist advice should be obtained on the latest developments and applications.

—   quick reference collection including bibliographical near catalogue.

—   general and special reference material.

—   reserved book collection, for example, in educational/academic institution.

—   material centralised or dispersed, for example, specialised departments with combined lending and reference stock.

—   telephone information service.

Determine:

—   types and approximate quantities of materials to be accommodated (books, records, tapes) and whether in separate spaces or zones.

— to what extent use will be made of computer and facsimile transmission systems etc.

Reading/study areas

Consider what forms of reading and study facilities should be included. Also, which require separate spaces and which should be combined with lending, reference or other services:

— periodicals and newspapers.
— large reading areas or a number of small areas adjoining subject bookstacks.
— separate reading/study areas for a particular class of user: academic staff, research workers, postgraduate students.
— carrels of different kinds.
— group study areas, seminar room(s), smoking-room.
— seats at windows with view, lounge chairs, outdoor reading areas.

Determine:

— what types of audio-visual equipment are to be provided.
— location of the equipment.

See 2.24.1.
Obtain specialist advice on the latest developments and applications of audio-visual equipment in reading/study areas: dial access systems and listening equipment, individually controlled players, microform readers, videotape viewers, computer consoles etc. For more detailed information see Appendix A.1.b: Brawne[7], Thompson[2] and Ellsworth[3].

Special collections

Ascertain whether a separate room with a higher than usual degree of security will be required for a special collection or valuable material:

— rare books and/or maps.
— manuscripts and archives.
— public documents.
— expensive art books.

See 2.24.1; also Appendix A.1.b: Ellsworth[3].

Special facilities

Consider what special/technical facilities are to be provided:

— closed-circuit television/video reproduction.
— tape and record listening facilities.
— microform viewing, document copying, typing etc.

Determine:

— which of them, if any, need separate spaces.
— which can be accommodated in one or more of the main spaces, for example in lending or reference departments.

See 2.24.1 and 2.24.2.
See Appendix A.1.b: Ellsworth[3] for examples from many university libraries. Obtain specialist advice on the latest equipment and systems.

Associated activities

Decide whether provision is to be made to accommodate various social/cultural activities: meetings, lectures, exhibitions etc. List anticipated activities (remember that requirements will change over the years) and determine:

— which require separate spaces.
— which can be accommodated in one or more general purpose rooms.

See 2.24.1.

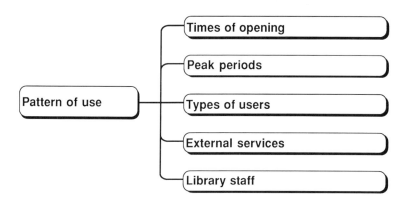

Times of opening

Determine opening times and implications for design. These may affect not only rostering and, therefore, numbers of staff, but also the system of control:
— number of days open each week.
— opening times for each day.
— what departments will remain open during evening hours.
— use of spaces for associated activities, for example, lecture and meeting-rooms in relation to library opening hours.

Peak periods

Assess the maximum expected number of users for each separate section of the library, and the times at which peak periods are likely to occur. Consider:
— the total number of students and teaching staff in educational institutions; also, the lecture and examination timetables.
— in the case of public libraries: types of readers (see below), location of library, total population of area to be served.

Types of users

Ascertain the anticipated types of users, the numbers of each and the proportion of male to female:
— adults, elderly, adolescents.
— children: special provision may be required – separate entrance, toilets.
— students and teaching staff.
— disabled persons and blind persons: special consideration will have to be given to ramps, lifts, door widths, lavatories, bypass of control turnstiles etc.
— extent of use, by local clubs or associations, of facilities such as meeting- and lecture-rooms.
Establish anticipated growth in numbers of each type of user and change in types of users.

External services

Consider whether the library will cater for any external services that may affect the number of staff required or that may have design implications:

— supply and services to branch, school or welfare libraries.
— mobile library service.
— links with other educational, social or cultural institutions including adult education groups.

Library staff

Determine staff structure according to activities, responsibilities, numbers and sexes:

— senior qualified staff librarian, deputy librarian, assistant librarians, library assistants, cataloguers.
— clerical: secretaries, typists, ordering and accounts clerks.
— technical: binding, photographic and photocopying.
— maintenance and cleaners.
— caretaker.

No general staffing levels can be laid down: requirements will be based on the population of the community to be served, the volume of use, and the range of services provided. Advice may be obtained from the local Library Association. Staffing costs represent a large proportion of the annual budget for providing a library service. Building design must afford the opportunity for economic staffing, for example providing the minimum number of control points.

2.10 Administrative and work areas

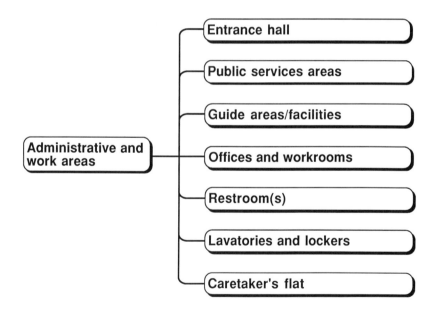

See 2.24.4.
For general information on internal circulation see Appendix A.1.a: *New Metric Handbook*[8], chapter 6.

The main control and service counter (or counters if separate for adults and children) should be visible from the entrance: users should be made immediately aware of the existence and function of all facilities the library has to offer.

See 2.24.2.
Obtain specialist advice on latest developments in issuing systems (computer systems), and electronic exit control equipment. See Appendix A.1.a: Thompson[2], chapter 10 and Ellsworth[3].
Control/supervision method will be related to that used for book storage (open or closed access) – see 2.11.
Small public libraries may be designed with all activities radiating from a central information/media counter.

See 2.24.2.
Specialist advice should be obtained on the latest developments in cataloguing systems and equipment. For more detailed information see Appendix A.1.a: Thompson[2], chapter 10 and Brawne[7].

Entrance hall

Establish how public is to be managed, directed to facilities, served, informed and supervised. Consider:

— circulation routes through entrance hall and access to public areas on all levels.

— position of main control/service counter in relationship to entrance hall.

— direct access to other areas: cloaks, lavatories, exhibition space, refreshment facilities, bookshop.

— other facilities to be provided: windbreaks (vestibule lobby), building directory, seating, display, notice-boards, publicity material (leaflet or pamphlet racks), vending-machines, coin-operated public telephone, chute or depository for return of books when library is closed, parking of prams and pushchairs.

Public service areas

Determine requirements for book issue and return counters (including system to be used), security/supervision points, readers' enquiry desks etc and the number of staff on duty in each of the sections/departments of the library:

— adults' lending and children's departments.

— reference and the various reading areas.

— special areas and subject departments (humanities, sciences etc. in university library).

Consider at which points, if any, turnstiles or other exit control devices will be required.

Guide areas/facilities

Establish what form of catalogue and other guides to library stock will be used and where they should be positioned:

— card or sheaf catalogue; computerised or microform system.

— single catalogue in central position; separate catalogues in main departments; computer consoles or microform readers in various locations.

Consider:

— whether general collection of reference material including bibliographies is to be located near catalogue.

— relationship of catalogue to enquiry desk.

— tables for consultation of card drawers.

— allowance for expansion.

Offices and workrooms

Ascertain administrative and technical personnel numbers, their activities and the accommodation required:

— executive and administrative offices – chief librarian, deputy librarian, offices for lending, reference and children's departments.
— committee room – separate or part of librarian's office.
— secretarial and clerical staff.
— areas for accessioning, cataloguing, processing, unpacking and dispatch.
— workrooms and studios – binding and repair, photographic, printing and duplicating, maintenance.

Determine:

— which people/functions require separate offices/workspace and which can share space.
— required relationship between personnel/functions: for which is adjacency important/unimportant?
— space requirements including storage.
— special requirements: safe/strongroom, equipment and machinery.

See 2.24.2.

The IFLA concludes that there is, generally speaking, a close relationship between the floor areas of the public departments and the space required for offices and workrooms: the floor area of the latter is usually approximately 20 per cent of the total floor area of the public departments. This in turn is approximately equivalent to 10-12 m² of office or workroom space per staff member.

Specialist advice should, however, be obtained on new methods of processing books – including computerised services – as these, if used, may affect the space requirements for some departments.

Restroom(s)

What type and scale of rest accommodation is required for staff?

— one lounge-like space with facilities for tea-making and simple food-preparation.
— or separate spaces (each with kitchen facilities) for different groups: professional, sub-professional and clerical staff on one hand, and the general, technical and maintenance staff on the other.

See 2.24.2.

Lavatories and lockers

Determine requirements for lavatories and locker facilities:

— separate provision for males and females or shared facilities.
— space requirements and number and type of lockers, WCs, urinals and wash-basins.
— changing areas and showers.
— small private rest area for women staff adjoining lavatory area.

See 2.24.2, also Appendix A.1.a: *New Metric Handbook*[8], chapter 38.

Caretaker's flat

Is a flat for a caretaker to be included as part of the library complex? If so, determine:

— space requirements.
— relationship to other areas and preferred position (for example, direct access from outside).

2.11   Material and storage

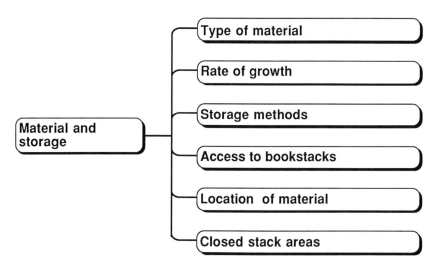

```
                                    ┌─────────────────────────────┐
                                    │  Type of material           │
                                    └─────────────────────────────┘
                                    ┌─────────────────────────────┐
                                    │  Rate of growth             │
                                    └─────────────────────────────┘
                                    ┌─────────────────────────────┐
  ┌──────────────┐                  │  Storage methods            │
  │ Material and │                  └─────────────────────────────┘
  │ storage      │                  ┌─────────────────────────────┐
  └──────────────┘                  │  Access to bookstacks       │
                                    └─────────────────────────────┘
                                    ┌─────────────────────────────┐
                                    │  Location  of material      │
                                    └─────────────────────────────┘
                                    ┌─────────────────────────────┐
                                    │  Closed stack areas         │
                                    └─────────────────────────────┘
```

Type of material

The IFLA recommends a minimum bookstock (covering all departments) of 9,000 volumes, that is, at least 3 volumes per inhabitant for small public libraries. In libraries for larger populations (above 60,000) a satisfactory general standard is 2 volumes per inhabitant.

Approximately one third of the total stock will be for children (up to 14 years) in relation to the total population.

A basic provision of at least 50 periodicals and newspapers is considered necessary.

The standard recommended for records and/or tapes is not less than 2,000 for a population of up to 20,000.

No standards are suggested for the provision of other materials.

Determine types, sizes and quantities of materials to be accommodated at opening of library:

— books – approximate number required for each operational section (adult lending, reference, children's department or subject division in university library). Also, the proportions of those under and over 250 mm tall and those which need to be laid flat (those over approximately 500 mm tall).

— periodicals – number of current issues to be displayed and back issues to be stored bound and/or unbound.

— newspapers – numbers of current issues to be displayed and method of storing back issues (in bound volumes or microform).

— pamphlets, sheet music, maps, manuscripts, clippings, photographs, pictures and prints.

— gramophone records, tapes (audio and video), films, slides, film strips and microforms.

Rate of growth

The IFLA recommends a minimum annual addition of 250 volumes per 1,000 of population, and a total of at least 300 records and/or tapes. Of total bookstock (that is 2 to 3 volumes per head of population) not less than one volume per head should be allocated to adult lending. It can be expected that about one third of this stock will be on loan at any one time, and part of the stock may be distributed to other service points such as a branch library.

Ascertain anticipated annual rate of acquisition of the various types of material and determine provision that must be allowed (at outset) for future expansion. Consider:

— basis of selection of new material: whether emphasis is to be on subject or on type of material.

— policy and method of purchasing material: continuous flow or sporadic.

— anticipated discard rate and effect on net growth.

— anticipated lending rate and estimated number of books on loan at any one time.

— policies on permanent preservation, for example, periodical files.

Storage method

Determine what method of storage will be used for the different types of material:

— by subject, size or type of material.

— type, height and depth of shelving units for books, periodicals etc.

— special storage requirements, for example, type of cabinets for microforms, maps etc.

See 2.24.3.

Access to bookstacks

Determine type of bookstack (area set aside primarily for storage of books and other library material) and degree of accessibility required in different sections of the library:

— open access – material freely available to users with storage units laid out to allow fairly spacious browsing conditions.

— open stack – material freely available to users but storage units in formal rows with minimum of browsing space.

— closed stack – access for staff only and material stored as closely as possible.

— if combinations are to be used (for example, mainly open access with some closed stack) establish proportions.

See 2.24.3.
Obtain specialist advice on the latest developments in microforms and ultramicroforms. The increased use of these and other telecommunication systems could reduce the space requirements for bookstacks.
For detail information see Appendix A.1.a: Brawne[7], Ellsworth[3,4] and Thompson[2].
The accessibility of the stacks to the public and the system of control used, will have a significant influence on the basic layout of the library.

Location of material

Establish where all the different types of material are to be located and what proportions of each are to be housed in each location:

— if open access or open stack – in which sections of the library: adult lending, reference, children's department, special collections etc.

— local closed stacks – separate stacks for individual sections of the library.

— general closed stacks.

As a general rule the IFLA recommends that in public libraries open access be provided for 600 volumes per 1,000 of population (Note: this takes into account books on loan and distributed to other service points – see 'Rate of growth' above), with a minimum of 4,000 volumes. For larger populations fewer books per 1,000 will be needed, for example: 60,000-80,000 provide 550 volumes per 1,000; 80,000-100,000 provide 500 volumes per 1,000.

Closed stack areas

Establish what type of closed stack is required:

— will limited access be required for any part of it – limited to a certain class of user or to certain times of day.

— multi-level with minimum horizontal distances or large in plan on minimum number of levels.

— central bookstack surrounded by public service areas.

— consider need for book lift or mechanical conveyor for vertical and horizontal transport of material.

— compact storage if space is limited: minimum circulation, rolling stacks etc.

— special requirements: for example, in Denmark main stack is usually in basement and planned to serve as an air-raid shelter.

See 2.24.3.
Also Appendix A.1.b: Thompson[2], chapters 8, 9 and 12, Brawne[7] and Ellsworth[3].

2.12 Ancillary areas

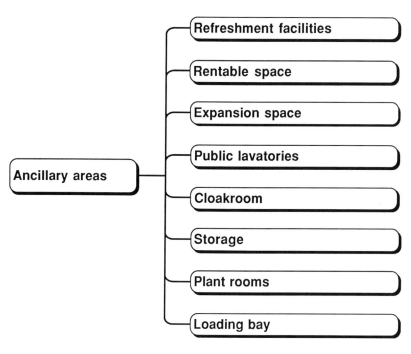

Refreshment facilities

See 2.24.4.
For detailed guidance see Appendix A.1.b: *New Metric Handbook*[8], chapter 20 and Lawson[9].
Information on local requirements should be obtained from the health department of the local authority.
In the UK see Food Hygiene (General) Regulations, 1970.

Consider need for, and scale/type of refreshment facilities:
— coffee bar or cafeteria/restaurant and/or vending-machines.
— form of service: waitress or counter.
— number of seats required.
— how service will be run, for example, leased to a private enterprise.
— hours of opening: will facility need to be located so that it can operate when library is closed, for example, with separate outside entrance?
— accessibility from library itself – from entrance lobby and not from main areas.
Establish what ancillary facilities are required:
— kitchen and/or other food preparation facilities; washing-up area etc.
— store(s) for kitchen and/or vending-machines.
— door to outside service area; refuse disposal.

Rentable space

A rare example of a bookshop inside a public library can be seen at Shoreditch Library in London.

Consider whether rentable space should be provided, for example, for a bookshop. If so, determine scale and scope of architect's responsibilities.

Expansion space

Ascertain whether provision should be made at outset for future expansion. If so, consider:

— what the space is to be used for in the meantime: offices, lecture rooms etc.

— special requirements: separate outside entrance, lavatory facilities etc.

Public lavatories

Decide whether public lavatories will be required. If so, determine:

— numbers – males, females and children – for whom provision must be made.

— location, for example: within main service core area so that readers do not have to pass through exit control; and/or adjacent to entrance hall if refreshment and/or general public facilities – lecture rooms, meeting rooms – are also to be served.

— special requirements for disabled persons and possibly children.

See 2.24.4; also Appendix A.1.b: *New Metric Handbook*[8], chapter 38.
Because of the problem of vandalism many librarians are against the provision of lavatory facilities in public libraries.

Cloakroom

Consider necessity for cloakroom in conjunction with measures for security of bookstock, that is, exclusion of bags and briefcases from library areas. If cloakroom is to be provided determine:

— type of facility – attendant or self-service – and number to cater for.

— type of storage for both outdoor clothing (hats and coats) and bags/briefcases: coatracks (possibly lockable type if self-service is used), lockers.

Alternatively, establish requirements for coatracks in library areas close to readers' seats.

See 2.24.4; also Appendix A.1.b: *New Metric Handbook*[8], chapter 38.
It is often difficult to persuade people – especially students – to make use of unattended cloakrooms close to the entrance. An attendant service, on the other hand, is expensive. Also, attendant cloakrooms do not generally function satisfactorily when large numbers of users arrive and leave at the same time as in university libraries.

Storage

Determine exact requirements for storerooms:

— list items to be stored: furniture (display screens, stacking chairs etc); stationery; cleaners' equipment and materials; packing materials; refuse.

— sizes of material and equipment; method of storage.

See 2.24.4.

Plant rooms

Determine need for, and approximate space requirements of:

— gas meter; oil storage tank; LPG installation (usually outside the building).

— boilers and other space heating plant.

— ventilation/air treatment plant.

— electrical sub-station and emergency installation.

— water storage tanks.

Consider location of spaces:

— basement.

— ground level.

— roof.

Discuss with specialist consultants, manufacturers etc. at early stage. See 2.24.4.

Loading bay

Determine need for loading bay for delivery of incoming material and dispatch of outgoing material. Consider:

— undercover facility or, if flush with outside wall, proprietary loading bay shelter which seals flush against outer surface of the vehicle body.
— platform and/or dock leveller.
— whether facility will be used for mobile library vehicle(s). If so, enclosed loading bay may be required to double as garage.

2.13   General considerations

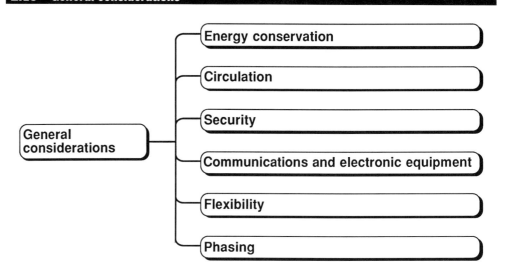

Energy conservation

See Appendix A.1.b: 'Energy Primer'[10].

Consider energy requirements and possible conservation:

— what fuel(s) will be used?
— solar energy; heat pump.
— could building be connected into a district heating system?

Circulation

See Appendix 1.A.b: Goldsmith[11] and *New Metric Handbook*[8], chapter 6.

Check on required pattern of movement through building for:

— the users – give special consideration to needs of disabled persons and mothers with prams: passage widths; escape routes from upper floors; ramps and gradients.
— the staff: staff entrance; staff only lifts for use with book trolleys.
— the materials: goods entrance; progress through processing; retrieval from and return to bookstack.

Security

Ascertain broad requirements with regard to:

— number and position of exits and fire escapes.

— fire alarms; firefighting installation and/or equipment.

— burglar alarms.

— anti-vandalism measures.

Discuss with local fire department and police. See Appendix A.1.b: 'Thinking About Fire'[12] and 'Security in Buildings'[13].

Communications and electronic equipment

Ascertain what provision must be made for:

— internal telephone/intercom system; also external telephones for both staff and public.

— closed-circuit television; computer consoles; facsimile transmission equipment, telex.

See Appendix A.1.b: Corby[14] and 'Communications'[15].
Discuss with telephone authority and relevant consultants/specialists (manufacturers/suppliers of electronic equipment).

Flexibility

Determine extent of planning for flexibility/adaptability and growth:

— to meet the estimated needs of the next 10-20 years.

— to allow, as far as possible, for future change in communication technology and other probable changes.

Consider:

— modular planning – freedom to use any part of building for almost any purpose – as opposed to fixed function spaces.

— provision of expansion space at outset.

— effect on structure and distribution of services.

It is not, generally speaking, realistic to consider providing total flexibility – the cost of services and the structure (designed to carry bookstacks anywhere) to do this would be extremely high. It is, therefore, important to decide what degree of flexibility is really essential.

Phasing

If library complex is to be built in stages, consider:

— priorities for each element/section.

— method of planning to permit building to remain in use continuously.

2.14 Site

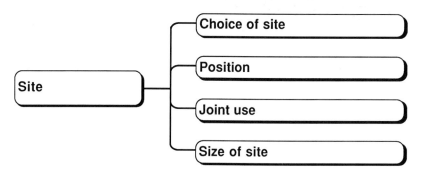

Choice of site

See Appendix A.2 for information on analysing chosen site or evaluating possible sites.
When considering cost of site keep the following in mind in addition to initial outlay:
– rates and taxes.
– effect of topography, soil conditions etc. on building and landscaping costs.
– possible cost of providing certain services on site.

If site has already been chosen check that:
— client has ascertained that it is suitable.
— alternatives have been investigated.
— general survey and feasibility have been undertaken.
— outline planning approval has been obtained.
If site has not yet been selected, investigate possible alternatives.

Position

Check/ensure that the site is:
— in a central and prominent position adjacent to other activities: shopping, entertainment etc.
— safely and easily accessible – by foot, bicycle, car and public transport – from all parts of the area it is to serve.
— of a suitable shape (for example, to allow correct orientation) and not too close to sources of noise or other disturbance.

Joint use

Public libraries are sometimes combined with other cultural or community facilities, or integrated into a shopping centre. They may, alternatively, be joint use, for example, general public and school. This may lead to greater use and possible savings: joint projects (exhibitions, for example), and sharing of servicing, parking, entrance etc.

If joint use or part of complex of buildings check that library can be so sited that:
— it will be clearly and easily indentified by users.
— there is no conflict with other uses.
Establish relationship to other buildings, for example, in university development.

Size of site

Establish that site is large enough for:
— estimated accommodation.
— future expansion, parking, outdoor reading areas and landscaping.
— if parking is not to be provided on site is there adequate parking in the immediate vicinity?

Feasibility

This phase is concerned with a study and analysis of the data collected in the initial brief in order to reach a decision on the feasibility of the project. If feasibility has already been established before the architect is appointed, this stage should be used to check the client's assessment and conclusions, and to ensure that no factors have been omitted.

The depth of analysis and design sufficient to prove feasibility may vary considerably. The factors included here are only the basic essentials; where a more thorough study is required the more detailed information given under 'Outline proposals/scheme design' (p.74) should be used.

See Appendix A.1.a: 'Plan of Work', Stage B in *Architect's Job Book*.

2.15 Appointments: architects/consultants

If it has not already been done the architect and consultants selected for the design phase should be formally appointed.
Agree to:
—   clear definitions of roles and responsibilities of all concerned.
—   services to be provided by each member of the design team.
—   scale of charges.

A design team containing people experienced in dealing with library buildings can contribute to smooth running of the project. Approach relevant professional bodies for advice.

2.16 Preliminary planning

Schedule of accommodation

An outline schedule of accommodation will have been drawn up during the previous stage (see p.50). Now:
—   check schedule, compare accommodation with known examples.
—   determine floor areas for each of the individual spaces.

For basic information on floor areas see 2.24. 1-4.

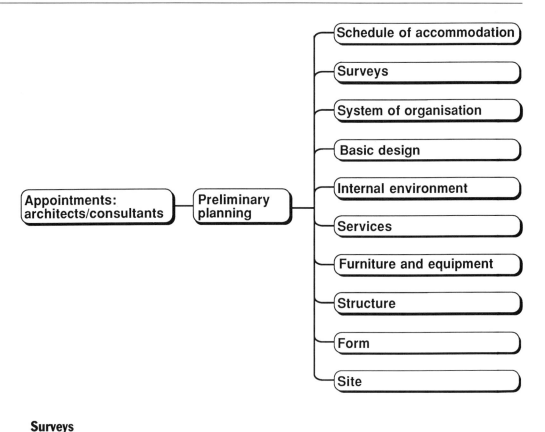

```
Appointments:          Preliminary       ┌─ Schedule of accommodation
architects/consultants  planning         ├─ Surveys
                                          ├─ System of organisation
                                          ├─ Basic design
                                          ├─ Internal environment
                                          ├─ Services
                                          ├─ Furniture and equipment
                                          ├─ Structure
                                          ├─ Form
                                          └─ Site
```

Surveys

For list of references see Appendix A.1.b. Useful sources include AJ 'Annual Review' (including bibliography) and AJ 'Guide to Information Sources'; also 'Architectural Periodicals Index' (RIBA).

Identify sources of information:
— survey current literature specifically relevant to project.
— prepare a list of references as a working document.
— investigate/visit related projects: pre-plan – know what to look for and why; carefully select buildings to visit (ideally, good examples of reasonably comparable type and size).

System of organisation

See Appendix A.5 for outline information on interaction matrices, etc.

Confirm which system of organisation is to be used in the new building:
— centralised or decentralised (as in university library).
— division of material by subject or by form and function.
— technical services, for example, cataloguing method.

Prepare:
— flow charts of activities, for example, progress of books from delivery to being borrowed by users, and pattern of operations within each major section/department.
— interaction/relationship matrix.

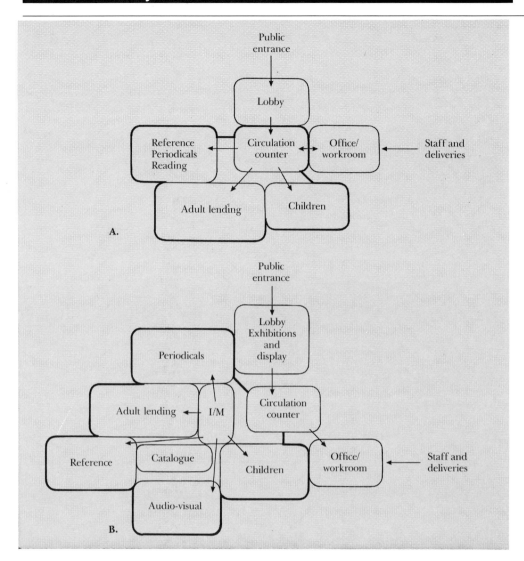

Fig. 2.2 *Simplified diagrams of some possible layouts in small public libraries. A. A single-room library with functions generally separated only notionally by furniture and/or layout (for example, L- or U-shaped space). B. In larger one-room libraries an information-media counter (I/M) may be included in a central location with all activities radiating from it. The counter usually features several staff/user services in one location, for example, bibliographies, data terminals and audio-visual machines (microreaders, viewers, players etc.).*

Basic design

Work out approximate form of building. Prepare several alternatives. Consider:

— building regulations and other special legislation affecting siting, design and construction.

— zoning: relationship between main elements of complex.

— vertical or horizontal organisation: if vertical, which areas on same level(s) as main entrance and goods entrance?

— visual relationships: control and supervision of public areas; spaces requiring privacy etc.

— relationship of layout to number of staff available: multi-level scheme will require staff at each level.

— circulation of users, staff and materials – entrances, corridors, vertical circulation, book conveyors etc – for greatest possible economy of effort.

See Figs 2.2, 2.3, 2.4.
For basic information on space and activity relationships see 2.24.1-4.
There should be no premature bias towards one single solution. Alternative solutions should, at this stage, be kept geometric.
Care must be taken with windows which should be carefully located and designed: obtain maximum effect from them, but keep glass areas to a minimum to conserve energy.

Fig. 2.3 *Simplified diagrams of some possible basic layouts in larger libraries. A. Public library. B. Academic library.*

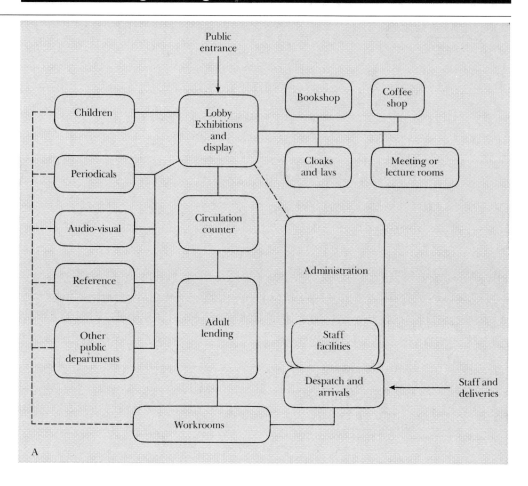

A

— external access: for users arriving on foot, by bicycle or car; position of areas needing direct vehicular access, for example, deliveries, mobile library.

— noise: position of noisy machines, for example, computer printout, telex; noisy stairwells; circulation patterns in and around reading areas; external sources (for example, traffic).

— orientation: in terms of heat gain and loss; view; external noise sources; prevailing winds (for example, windows and entrances).

— fenestration: general percentages in different facades. How will this affect ventilation, daylight, heat gain and loss, construction and appearance? Reading areas in relation to windows, for example, around perimeter of building.

— flexibility and phasing: degree of modular planning (see also internal environment, services and structure below); position of areas to be added, or spaces to be extended, in the future.

— relationship with adjoining facilities.

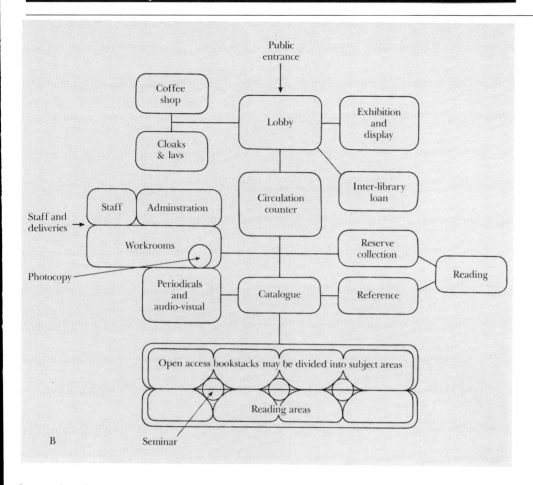

Internal environment

Consider broad requirements for:

— air-conditioning: heating, cooling, ventilation, humidification, de-humidification, filtering and washing; also space requirements for plant, trunking etc.

— if no air-conditioning: mechanical ventilation with heating in winter. What will be done to ensure there is no overheating during hot summer months?

— lighting.

— acoustic control: double glazing, absorbent ceilings, floor finish, orientation, layout etc.

Determine:

— zones for air-conditioning, heating etc; consider effect of fenestration.

— whether smoking will be permitted in parts of the building.

— whether there are any special requirements for a computer or other electronic equipment.

— flexibility/adaptability required: the degree to which atmospheric and comfort conditions and lighting must be suitable for both books and users.

— the degree to which internal energy will be recycled, for example, waste heat recovery.

Consult appropriate specialists, manufacturers and suppliers.
Deterioration of paper in particular is a problem. Not only must air be free from dust and pollution but it must also be maintained at fairly constant levels of temperature and humidity to ensure preservation of library material.
See also 2.24.3.

Fig. 2.4 *Basic flow patterns of main library materials. The workrooms shown may not be provided (for example, withdrawals may be part of accessions) and in a small public library all operations are generally performed in a single workroom.*

Accessions: Bibliographic checking and ordering of material recommended for purchase; to receive and account for incoming material.
Catalogue: To classify and catalogue material and maintain bibliographic records.
Typists/Punch operators: Produce catalogue cards or tape for computer input.
Processing: Preparing books for shelves: marking spines, applying labels, pockets, diodes (for electronic exit control) etc.; may do mending of books and preparation for binding.
Withdrawals: Preparation of books for binding and withdrawal of books to be disposed of, etc.
Periodicals (serials): To receive, catalogue and prepare all periodicals, newspapers, etc.; preparing material for binding and microfilming.

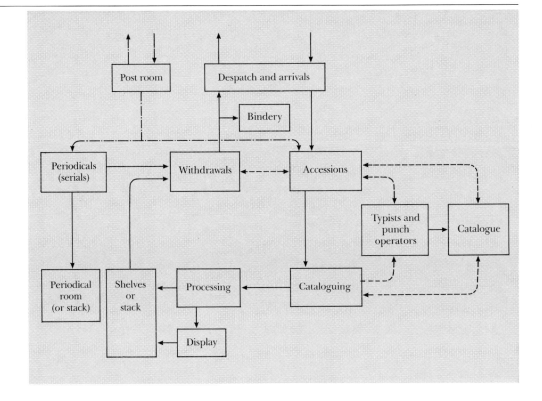

Discuss with local authorities/supply boards etc. The location of plant rooms and main distribution runs (vertical and horizontal) must be considered together with the structure at an early stage if services are to be satisfactorily integrated.

Investigate alternatives which will be most appropriate for:
— each of the layouts selected.
— the different types of spaces.
— the structural systems under consideration.

Services

Ensure that adequate supply and disposal services will be available:
— water supply and electricity: will a transformer be required? If so, how much space will be needed?
— waste disposal: how much waste accumulates weekly? How will it be stored and removed?

Consider:
— communication systems (internal and external telephones, teleprinters, tube transmission systems etc.) including floor space and other requirements: location, power, air-conditioning etc.
— protection systems (for example, fire) and effect on design.
— integration and distribution of services: position of distribution boards and plant rooms to keep runs to a minimum; compatability with structural systems.
— flexibility, for example, for wiring – power, telephone cables, coaxial cables etc.

Furniture and equipment

Ascertain what fixed and loose furniture and equipment must be included. Check:
— dimensions and weights.
— methods of fixing.
— costs.

The furniture and equipment to be used can have a significant influence on planning, structure and cost. Consult manufacturers/suppliers.

Structure

Investigate structural possibilities for the various layouts. Consider:

See 2.24.3.

— column grid: this is a crucial decision to ensure economic use of space and maximum adaptability; must be worked out in terms of bookstacks (shelving and aisle dimension), table and chair layouts (reading areas), and workstation dimensions.
— floor loadings, for example, provision for conventional or compact/mobile bookstacks throughout, or in predetermined areas only.
— height of building and storey heights: preferred floor-to-ceiling height which should be chosen with regard to bookstack heights plus allowance for light fittings and comfort of readers/users. Keep air circulation in mind.
— distribution of services: flat slab with suspended ceiling or other system.

Form

Develop the massing of the various layouts (probable building shape) and relate to site and adjacent buildings.
Consider:
— whether requirements of internal spaces – form/volume and relationships – have been taken into account.
— suitability for function and image to be projected.
— suitability for expansion either vertical or horizontal.
— suitability for either air-conditioning or natural ventilation, and natural lighting.
— heat loss and gain: cubic form may be better than elongated/thin building or high-rise.
— town planning regulations.
— cost: economy of surface to volume ratio.

Site

Check that each of the layouts fits the site. Keep in mind:
— adequate access for users and suppliers.
— future expansion.
— outdoor requirements, for example, in a university library relationship to main circulation routes between departments – covered links may be needed.

2.17 Cost planning

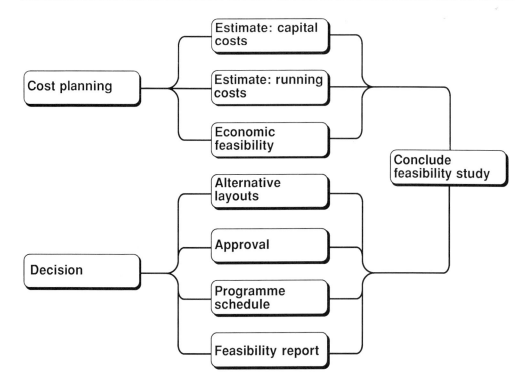

Estimate: capital costs

Obtain estimates of capital costs of alternative layouts from quantity surveyor; include all professional fees and expenses.

Estimate: running costs

Prepare outline of probable running costs. Consider:
— alternative solutions with regard to operational methods and likely effect on running costs, for example, numbers of staff needed.
— maintenance of building and services.
— energy consumption: fuel for lighting, heating etc.
— likely income if any.

Economic feasibility

Balance financial needs and resources; determine economic feasibility.

2.18 Conclude feasibility study

Alternative layouts

On the basis of foregoing studies and comparative analysis:
— select best alternative solution to building layout.
— prepare final proposal based on several alternatives.

Discuss alternatives with all interested parties. No one layout may represent a solution; several may confirm criteria which final solution requires.

Approval

Obtain approval of development in principle from local authority.

Programme schedule

Prepare revised programme schedule. Determine:
— earliest and latest dates for starts and completions for each aspect of work.
— resource implications affecting programme, for example, finance.

Check sequence of operations with all members of design and client team. Discuss implications and adjust overall programme and resource allocations if necessary to balance time needed with time available.

Feasibility report

Prepare report on feasibility of project, including proposals, in terms of:
— client's stated requirements.
— site limitations.
— complete financial implications making clear relative allocation of costs to building fabric, services, furniture and fittings, landscaping, professional fees etc.
— structure, services etc.
Note any modifications that should be made to the brief.

Decision

Submit report for consideration to client. A decision must be taken:
— to proceed, or
— to modify requirements and reassess feasibility, or
— to abandon the project.

Detailed brief

See Appendix A.1.a: 'Plan of Work', Stage C in *Architect's Job Book*.

This phase is concerned with setting-out a detailed brief covering all the major factors with which those involved in the project must be concerned. It represents amplification of and addition to the broad issues discussed in the primary brief. In form it is usually written and diagrammatic and it emerges as a result of periods of extended talks with the client, the design team and the users.

Further design work may start before the completion of a full brief and certain studies under 'Outline proposals/scheme design' (p.74) may need to be made before the detailed brief can be substantially finalised. Obviously, this brief will require review and, inevitably, amendment and revision as the work progresses.

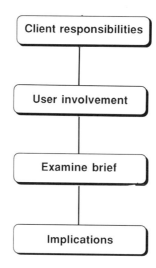

2.19 Client responsibilities

Ensure that the client provides, or helps to provide, data on detailed requirements. Discuss design implications, for example, in relation to operational and management policies.

2.20 User involvement

Ensure that the ideas developed up to this stage are made available to the local community or other users (for example, faculty and students) for comment and reaction.

This can be done through:

— the local press.
— an exhibition or leaflet.
— meetings.
— local clubs and societies.

It serves no useful purpose to publicise proposals when it is too late for future users to make a positive contribution. Participation by them in the production of the brief ensures commitment to the subsequent design and an understanding of the completed project.

2.21 Examine brief

Be sure to:

— check that all items listed under initial brief and feasibility have been considered.
— list any outstanding items about which decisions have yet to be reached or research initiated.
— examine basic changes in requirements for their effect on previous feasibility judgements (Note: costs).

The various specialists (including manufacturers or suppliers of specialised equipment) must be asked to consider the implications of the up-to-date brief as it affects their particular responsibilities.

2.22 Implications

Consider implications of the detailed brief with regard to:

— previous decision,
— contracting methods.
— the project programmes as a whole.

Revise the programme if necessary; advise the client and other relevant persons/bodies of any changes.

Outline proposals/ scheme design

See Appendix A.1.a: 'Plan of Work', Stages C and D (with the exception of part 2 'Architect's management function') in *Architect's Job Book*.

This phase determines the general approach to layout, design and construction, which is developed to the point where one definite scheme (together with cost analysis) is produced and agreed upon by all the consultants and put forward as a recommended solution to the client. This phase may well have been reached by the end of the feasibility period, and may therefore be the confirmation of an already fairly detailed solution but incorporate any modification found necessary while preparing the feasibility study and detailed brief.

If the feasibility phase was bypassed, the factors outlined in that phase should be consulted for a broad appreciation of the size of the problem and as a quick check on the feasibility of the client's more detailed requirements now available.

2.23   Detailed information

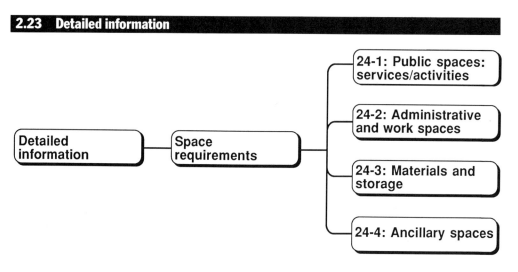

Studies undertaken in broad terms only at an earlier stage must now be carried out in detail:
— site studies.
— survey of user requirements.
— evaluation of similar projects etc.

2.24 Space requirements

Assess floor area and design requirements for individual spaces:
— services.
— administrative and work areas.
— material and storage.
— ancillary spaces.
For each space list:
— nature of activity performed there, for example, flow/circulation pattern; quiet or noisy; browsing or study.
— relationships to other spaces/functions.
— type and amount of materials to be housed; number of seats to be provided and staff to be accommodated.
— special requirements, for example, surveillance.
— furniture and fittings.
— requirements for services, lighting, heating, acoustics etc.
— provision for flexibility/adaptability and for expansion.
Sections 2.24.1-4 give the basic requirements for each individual space. To save undue repetition certain detailed information which may only be required during the following phase is included in these sections.

Basic information is given on each space considered. This is followed in each case by layout/design considerations with accompanying detail/technical information in the margin.

Note: standards must be seen as flexible guidelines to be adapted according to the type of library and local needs.

2.24.1 Public areas: services

Lending department: adults
This is normally the main service provided by a public library. Users to be encouraged to browse and select their own material from that stored and displayed on open-access units.

Bookstock in public libraries usually 2-3 volumes per inhabitant: of these at least 1 volume per inhabitant will be for adult lending, around ⅓ of which will be off the shelves at any one time.

Open-access shelving must, therefore, be provided for 600 volumes per 1,000 population served up to 60,000 (550 volumes per 1,000 for 60,000-80,000 and 500 volumes per 1,000 above this) with a suggested minimum of 4,000 volumes.

The IFLA recommends that $15\,m^2$ be provided for every 1,000 volumes on open shelves (units 5 shelves high) with a minimum of $100\,m^2$. For a medium-sized

Book shelving: units commonly 900 mm wide, approximately 2 m (5 shelves) high and 200-230 mm deep (300 mm for oversized books) per side. Number of fiction volumes per single-sided unit 75 per cent full = 120-130; non-fiction = 90-100. Island fittings usually double-sided units up to 1350 mm high. Height from floor to bottom shelf in all units, 300-400 mm minimum. See Figs 2.5, 2.6, 2.7.

Other fittings: for detailed information and advice consult specialist manufacturers/ suppliers.

Finishes and design should help to create a warm, informal and relaxed atmosphere: a soft flooring such as carpet can contribute towards this and help greatly to reduce the noise level.

Some wall surfaces may need to be suitable for displaying artwork; consider ease of maintenance, particularly of surfaces which can be touched by readers.

Lighting: main problem is to achieve a satisfactory level of lighting on vertical faces of bookshelves and other display units: 150 lux vertically at floor level. See also 'Bookstack' (p.79). Separate track lighting may be required for display of artwork.

Mechanical ventilation rate: 3-6 air changes per hour.

library, serving populations of 20,000-60,000, this is equivalent to providing about $9 \text{ m}^2/1,000$ population which allows for circulation space, counters and catalogues, informal seating (1/1,000 population) without table space and a moderate amount of display equipment. Additional space may be required if large amounts of other material (for example: records, cassettes, paintings, slides) are to be provided for. If space is to be used for exhibitions add around 10 per cent of floor area.

Allow for future expansion based on estimated rate of net annual acquisitions. In small to medium libraries other activities may be included, for example, children's department, reading areas, reference, periodicals, information/media centre. Space for these functions must be added – see under relevant headings below.

Should, ideally, have direct access from entrance hall and be designed to allow for maximum visual supervision from the circulation counter.

Layout of bookshelving is important. Consider:

— simple and logical arrangement, for clear and continuous sequence of books, for example, alphabetical for fiction and numerical for non-fiction; provide clear signage.

— provision for oversized material, paperbacks and non-book media.

— convenient traffic lines and ease of movement for borrowers and staff with trolleys, for example, spacing between island units 1.8 m approximately (keep wheelchair users in mind) at least 2.5 m if informal seating is to be allowed for.

— length of island shelving: if too short sequence is interrupted; if too long may cause obstruction. Shelving grouped in alcoves or bays is a possibility which provides degree of enclosure and privacy.

Seating should be close to books but must not prevent easy circulation particularly at busy times. A variety of seating types allows for flexibility – *see also* 'Reference' (p.79), 'Periodicals/Newspapers' (p.80) and 'Seating' (p.80).

Lending department: children

Provision is usually made for lending facilities (books and other materials), displays (new material, hobbies, art), reference material and study space which can be used for doing school homework. Accommodation may be included for individual and/or group listening to and viewing of audio-visual materials, and for library-sponsored activities such as story hours, talks, demonstrations, puppet shows and creative play. A separate room is often provided for some of these activities.

The number of books provided varies from country to country but generally speaking will be up to 25-30 per cent of total library bookstock. The IFLA recommends that 16 m^2 be allowed for each 1,000 volumes on open-access shelving (units 4 shelves high), that is $75\text{-}100 \text{ m}^2$ for total population up to 10,000; $100\text{-}200 \text{ m}^2$ for population of 10,000-20,000. This allows for circulation space, counters and catalogues, informal seating without tables and a moderate amount of display equipment. Space for study (tables and chairs) and special activities should be added.

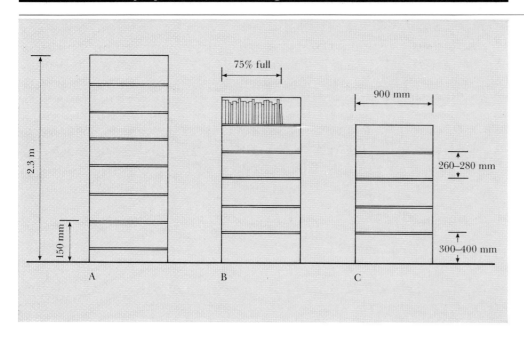

Fig. 2.5 *Book capacity of library shelving. For general estimating purposes assume an average of 125 volumes in a standard single-faced unit of shelving 900 mm wide and height as follows: 7 shelves for stack areas (A); 5 shelves for adult lending areas (B); and 4 shelves in children's departments. A book collection grows throughout (that is, at all points in the classification sequence) and space for expansion must therefore be provided on each shelf. The above figure is based on the following number of books per 900 mm (figures in all cases are for shelves approximately 75 per cent full):*

- *books for loan in a public library (fiction and non-fiction): 25–25*
- *children's books: 30–36*
- *reference/academic (history, science, technology, etc.): 18–19*

Note: A bookshelf is regarded as full when it contains approximately 85 per cent of its capacity; if fuller than this it is difficult to handle books and bindings may be damaged.

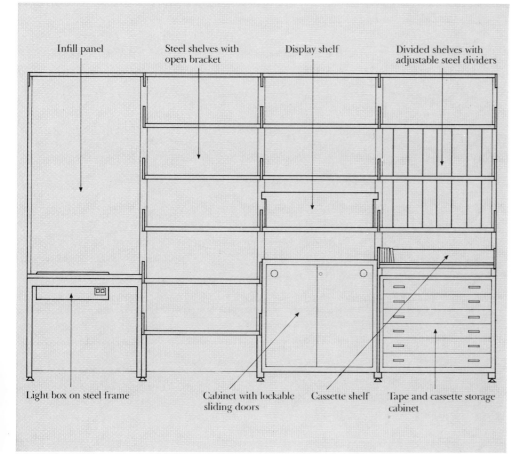

Fig. 2.6 *There are various proprietary modular library shelving/storage systems on the market. Illustrated above are the elements of a typical steel system based on wall strips, and single- and double-sided uprights which are all slotted at 25 mm centres. Shelves are in widths of 750 mm, 900 mm and 1 mm depths ranging from 200 to 500 mm.*

Fig. 2.7 *Typical layouts and shelf spacing in public libraries (adult lending and reference).*

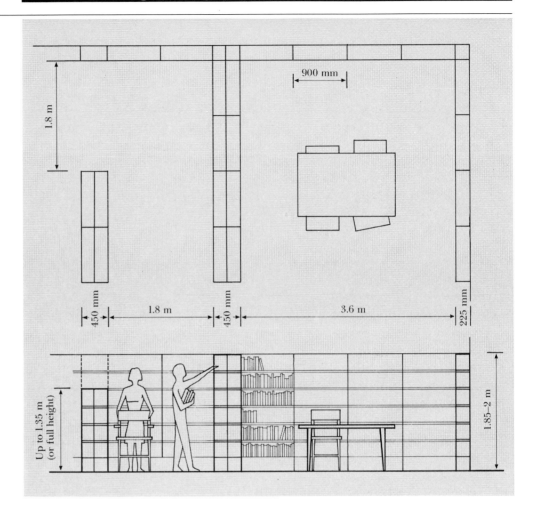

Book shelving: as for – 'Lending department: adults' (p.76) but maximum height 1.5-1.6 m (4 shelves).

Average number of books per single-sided unit = 120-130, except where books are displayed face forward – then 3-5 volumes per 900 mm of shelving. Height from floor to bottom shelf 75 mm minimum for very small children.

Other fittings: open bin units ('kinderboxes') may be used for oversized and thin picture-books and combined with low seating; bin units may be on wheels for flexibility.

For finishes, lighting and ventilation see 'Lending department: adults': (p.76).

Should, ideally, have direct access from entrance hall. Where it is part of adults' library plan space so that children pass circulation (control) desk to reach their area but without crossing adult section; children's space should be in full view of control staff. Where children's and adults' sections are in separate rooms allow for easy movement between them (for older children using adult section and parents taking out books for children etc).

Consider:

— location relative to areas needing quiet: children's library may be a source of noise at times.

— scale and atmosphere: ceiling height, sense of enclosure, size of furniture, lighting etc.

— variety of spaces and experiences: special corner for younger children; carpeted sunken area so that children can sit on step for story hour, individual listening to records and similar activities.

Reference

The reference section (stack and reading area) may be in a single space together with the adult lending department (small to medium public library), or in a separate space which, in addition to reference books, may contain periodicals, newspapers and audio-visual materials.

In open-access libraries divided into subject departments (for example, academic libraries) with reference material housed in each department, a general reference area and staff desk/counter is usually placed close to the catalogue. This area will contain bibliographies, directories and basic reference material.

Reference bookstock, which must be available at all times and cannot be borrowed, from 60-200 volumes per 1,000 population served (2-10 per cent of total stock) depending on size of library:

population	*volumes*
5,000	300
10,000	900
20,000	3,000
40,000	7,000
60,000	12,000

Allow $10\,m^2$ of floor space per 1,000 volumes on open shelves. Provide seating for between 1.5-2 persons per 1,000 population served (may be less: 1 seat per 1,000 for larger libraries) and allow $2.5\text{-}3\,m^2$ per reader space depending on type and arrangement of seats and tables. For a medium-sized library this is approximately equivalent to $6\text{-}7\,m^2$ of floor space per 1,000 population served and allows for circulation and staff counter space. If periodicals and/or audio-visual materials are included, space will need to be added for these functions – see 'Periodicals/ newspapers' (p.80) and 'Special collections/rooms' (p.83).

Generally a quiet area for concentrated work. Consider:

— system to be used, for example, in library divided into subject departments will reference stock and librarians be centralised or decentralised (that is, small general reference collection near catalogue and subject stock with related open-access collections)?

— quiet location relatively close to catalogue, and to public lavatories (if provided) as some readers may spend long periods working in this department.

— if applicable, position relative to closed stack and circulation/method of delivery between these spaces.

— layout: shelving around walls with seating in centre or freestanding shelving in centre and seating next to window walls etc.

— security, for example, visual supervision of space (this will influence layout) and exit control.

— position of office for reference librarian, if required, and location relative to staff desk/counter.

Book shelving: see 'Lending department: adults' (p.76).

Average shelf-to-shelf space will need to be greater than for lending department to allow for a larger proportion of oversized books such as encyclopedias, atlases and directories.

Audio-visual: special fittings/facilities may be required (see p.83).

Finishes: as for 'Lending department: adults' (p.76).

Lighting: 150 lux vertically at floor level for bookshelves and 500 lux on study tables. Special lighting may be required for audio-visual equipment etc. (see p.83). Mechanical ventilation rate: 3-6 air changes per hour.

Periodicals/newspapers

In many medium to large public libraries a separate periodicals and newspaper room is provided. Alternative solutions include keeping some (the more specialised/scientific) or all of the current periodicals and newspapers in the reference library. In open-access libraries divided into subject departments (for example, academic libraries) periodicals, both current and back issues, may be decentralised by subject and kept with related book collections.

The IFLA recommends a basic provision of at least 50 periodicals in public libraries and in medium to large units 10 periodicals per 1,000 population served. Provide one seat per 2,000 for populations up to 20,000 (1/3,000 above this); approximately $3\,m^2$ of floor space per reader should be adequate for tables and chairs as well as space to display current material.

Shelving/display: consider types of material to be provided for – current periodicals and newspapers, back issues (before they are bound) and bound volumes etc.
Various standard fittings are available. Check capacity, dimensions and practicality of each.
Finishes and mechanical ventilation rate: as for 'Lending department: adults' (pp.75-6).
Lighting: 300 lux on reading tables.
Note: special newspaper reading tables may be required.

Should ideally be near main entrance and easily accessible for all users. Users may need/want a place in the library where they can meet and talk: the periodicals/newspaper room can become a social centre.
Consider:
— the casual, possibly noisy, character of the space.
— the location relative to serials workroom (which may need to be close to the counter/exit control), reference department and photocopy facilities.
— if applicable, location relative to closed stack (possibly for bound volumes) and circulation/method of delivery between these spaces.
— provision of windows to outside.

Seating (reading/study areas)

Reading/study facilities may be provided in separate spaces, possibly for the exclusive use of a particular class of reader – research workers in a public library or academic staff in an academic library – or be distributed in small groups among bookshelves and display units.

Areas in which seating may be required include lending departments, reference, periodicals and newspapers, study areas in open-access bookstacks (for example, in academic libraries), special collections (rare books, audio-visual and microform departments), group study and/or seminar rooms.

A variety of seating types, ranging from provision for casual browsing to serious study, should be provided. The proportion will vary according to the location (department) and the type of library. Space allowances per reader vary according to the type of seating (areas given below include for part of main circulation):
— small easy chair: $2.3\,m^2$
— individual table (600 mm × 900 mm) and chair: $2.3\,m^2$
— 4-12 readers per table without dividers, depending on width of table, lateral allowance and spacing of tables: 1.4-$1.9\,m^2$
— individual open carrel (screened table): $2.8\,m^2$
— 4-12 readers per table with dividers: 2.2-$2.3\,m^2$
— 4 individual open carrels in pinwheel layout: 2.8-$3\,m^2$/place
— individual enclosed carrel (2.1 m × 1.7 m): $4.6\,m^2$
(Note: a smaller carrel – min 1.5 m × 1.3 m – may be used.)

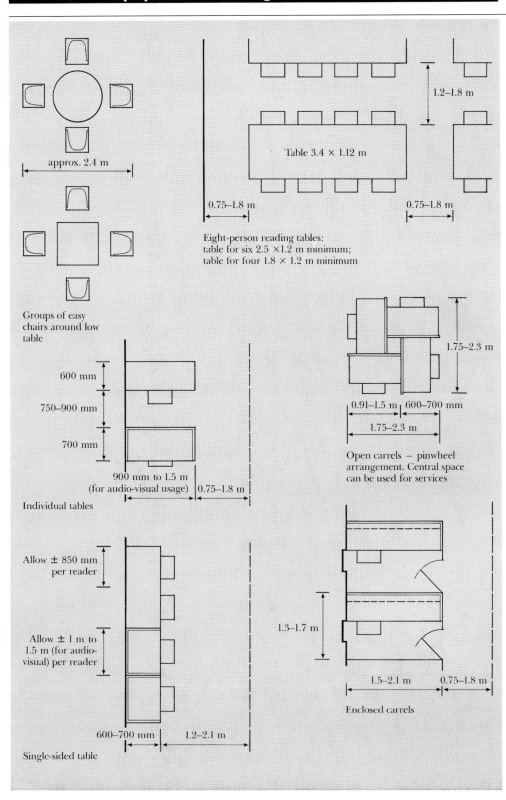

Fig. 2.8 *Space requirements for various types of seating and table arrangements. Height of study tables should be between 710 and 760 mm (635 – 700 mm for children); height of screens to open carrels approximately 1.3 m from floor.*

approx. 2.4 m

Groups of easy chairs around low table

Table 3.4 × 1.12 m

1.2–1.8 m

0.75–1.8 m 0.75–1.8 m

Eight-person reading tables:
table for six 2.5 ×1.2 m minimum;
table for four 1.8 × 1.2 m minimum

600 mm

750–900 mm

700 mm

900 mm to 1.5 m
(for audio-visual usage) 0.75–1.8 m

Individual tables

1.75–2.3 m

0.91–1.5 m 600–700 mm

1.75–2.3 m

Open carrels – pinwheel arrangement. Central space can be used for services

Allow ± 850 mm
per reader

Allow ± 1 m to
1.5 m (for audio-visual) per reader

1.3–1.7 m

1.5–2.1 m 0.75–1.8 m

Enclosed carrels

600–700 mm 1.2–2.1 m

Single-sided table

Furniture: chairs should be comfortable as readers may sit in the library for hours. Consider provision of a variety of types to allow for individual differences and to vary feeling in different areas.

Individual tables should be approximately 900 mm × 600 mm: size will need to be increased if audio-visual equipment (microreaders, television and computer consoles etc) is to be used.

At larger tables allow lateral space of between 800 mm-1 m per reader (up to 2 m for special materials, for example, maps) and depth of between 500-700 mm (up to 1 m for special material).

Space between parallel tables (or tables and shelves) 1.2-2 m. Surfaces of table tops should be relatively light in colour and have a matt finish. See Fig.2.8.

Open carrels: partitions should be 1,350 mm high (from floor) and where used for typing there should be acoustic screens. Enclosed carrels: should have lockable door and inspection window. Must be soundproof and well ventilated; view to outside desirable. Provide worktop, shelves and pinning board. See Fig.2.8.

Service outlets: consider flexible provision of outlets for headphones, microreaders, computer and television terminals etc. Trunking, possibly with vertical service poles, may provide solution.

Lighting: between 300-500 lux depending on task to be performed. Quality of lighting – free of direct glare, veiling reflections, shadows (for example, from carrel dividers) – is extremely important. Great care must be taken with design of installation and with selection of luminaires.

Ventilation: location of outlets important to ensure that there is no draught on readers.

Determine seating and table requirements (including proportions of different types) for each of the public areas.

There is no standard suitable for all academic libraries; seating is generally required for approximately 20 per cent of total student enrolment. Requirements will vary from department to department, for example, law students may require seating for up to 90 per cent of enrolment.

Consider the following:

— location of browsing and study places in relation to books and other materials, staff counters/stations, windows, circulation routes etc. Type and proportion of stack (open or closed access) will influence basic layout, for example, readers will need to be near catalogue in predominantly closed access system.

— location close to library materials but in such a way that people moving do not distract readers: maximum acceptable level of background noise 30-35 dB.

— location on perimeter walls: may have advantages, for example, daylight, views, easier to provide services, and economical use of space (if tables at right angles to walls and adjacent to aisles).

— degrees of enclosure and levels of privacy required: open seating for supervision, alcoves, open-carrels, closed-carrels etc.

— provision of lockers for papers and books close to open-carrels; facilities for hanging outdoor clothes close to seating and in the view of readers.

— provision of outdoor reading areas, for example, in enclosed courtyard.

Special collections/rooms (for example, audio-visual and microforms)

Collections of audio-visual and/or microform material which may be centralised –
either in a separate space with controlled access or together with another
department (for example, reference) – or decentralised into subject locations
together with related books and periodicals. If decentralised, reading machines
and other audio-visual equipment will have to be provided in various locations
throughout the library.

A special audio-visual department may include some, or all, of the following:
display, reference, circulation and counter areas; microform reading area;
individual listening/viewing stations; enclosed listening/viewing carrels or booths
for small groups; closed stack or open-access shelving (possibly behind grilles for
security) for reels of film, tapes, slides, microforms etc, and storage for equipment;
workroom; office and control booth. The floor area required will depend on system
used, facilities provided and seating required, and the amount and type of material
to be housed.

Must be closely related to audio-visual storage (materials and equipment) and to
photographic/graphic production facilities if these are included; may be linked to
reference area to reduce number of service/control points or, as in some public
libraries, to an information-media counter. Layout will be determined by system
used, facilities required etc.

Consider:

— method of storage and display of various materials: open access or behind
grille or closed access.
— system to be used for music listening: central console with headphone
outlets (and possibly dial access) at various points; tables with individual
players and headphones; soundproof booths and/or listening rooms for
small groups.
— system to be used for viewing: equipment containing own screen; small
screens as part of workstations; viewing booths/rooms for small groups
with wall-mounted screen, television receiver, space for equipment cart etc.
— Equipment: what will be kept permanently set up for use; what stored until
needed?

Furniture: a variety of special storage/display and workstation fittings will be needed. Specialist advice should be obtained; consult manufacturers for detailed information.

Equipment: determine what must be provided; consult manufacturers for detailed information and advice on special requirements.

Lighting: 150-300 lux at table or work level. Generally lighting should ideally be controlled by variable dimmer switches. Care must be taken with provision of light sources to prevent veiling reflections on screens: totally indirect system may be a solution. Consider flexible individually switched task lights at each workstation for note-taking.

Service outlets: flexible provision of cables and outlets for headphones, microreaders, computer consoles, television receivers etc.

Acoustics: in listening rooms (sound insulation, wall surfaces etc); obtain specialist advice. If stereo speakers are to be used space should be at least 3.1 m × 3.1 m with speakers placed far enough apart so that sounds mingle before they reach the ear.

Local studies

Collection of material (including books, periodicals, maps, photographs, prints,
slides) of local interest. May be part of lending or reference departments; often
housed in separate room in larger libraries. Area required will depend on amount
and type of material on open-access display and on the number and type of seats to
be provided.

Location will depend on type and size of library. Even if housed in separate space it
may be linked to reference department to reduce number of service/control points.
Layout will be determined by materials to be displayed and facilities to be
provided.

Requirements will depend on material displayed and facilities to be provided. See 'Special collections/rooms' above and 'Map rooms' (p.84).

Map rooms

Maps and atlases may be kept in reference department or in geographical subject division. In libraries with a large collection a separate room may be provided for storage/display as well as for special equipment for users to work on maps (to study, trace, enlarge or reduce them).

Counter and/or office space, and a workroom for map processing and repair may be required. Floor area will depend on amount and type of open-access display and equipment; also on the number and type of seats to be provided.

A variety of special furniture and equipment will be needed: light tables for map tracing, cabinets for horizontal or vertical storage of maps and for storage of atlases, large map tables, pantograph, projector, copier etc. Specialist advice should be obtained.
Lighting: 300-500 lux on working plane – possibly general lighting with adjustable individually switched task lighting for intensive study/detailed work.

Should be close to geographical subject division or reference department with which it may be linked to reduce number of service/control points. Location will be determined largely by weight of map cabinets: it may have to be on ground floor. Consider wall display of new maps and of those constantly referred to.

Music and/or art rooms

Collections of sheet music, records, tapes, pictures, slides etc, for loan or reference may be housed in lending and/or reference departments, in a separate audio-visual room, or in special subject rooms, for example, music room where all music material (including books) is concentrated. Area required will depend on the amount and type of material and equipment to be housed and the seating to be provided; additional area may be required for counter, office and/or workroom, and for special listening/viewing facilities.

Furniture and fittings: as for 'Reference' (p.79) and 'Audio-visual' (p.83). Rails or other system for hanging pictures on walls may be required.
Lighting: 300-500 lux on working plane. See also 'Audio-visual' (p.83). Directional lighting (for example, flexible spotlights on track) may be required for pictures and prints. Specialist advice should be obtained.
Service outlets and acoustics: see 'Audio-visual' (p.83).

Should be close to reference department with which room(s) may be linked to reduce number of service/control points.

Consider space requirements of special fittings and equipment required: where individual players, viewing machines and other equipment is to be used provide enough space for users to work (spread out music scores, take notes etc.). Decide on system of displaying/storing art collections if these are available for loan or reference: on wall or on hinged or sliding screens etc.

Rare books

Collections of manuscripts and archival material etc. These materials are usually kept in locked units or in a closed stack (where environmental conditions can be carefully controlled) adjacent to the special reading room. Area required will depend on amount of material to be housed, the seating to be provided, and any provision for counter and/or office from which the reading space can be kept under surveillance.

As for 'Seating (reading/study areas)' (p.80) – see also 2.24.4: 'Bookstacks'.
Display cases: need to be specially designed: provision for ventilation of cases with dust filters at air inlets; provision for stabilising relative humidity etc. Specialist advice should be obtained.
Lighting: tungsten filament spotlights should not be used; fluorescent tubes should have ultra-violet filtration.

Consider location and layout particularly in terms of control over access and surveillance of users. Determine system to be used: in some libraries readers are locked into the reading area and must hand in books before they leave. Consider how books and other material are to be displayed and stored: will some display/storage be required in public area?

Reserve department

Usually in academic libraries for special books: those for assigned reading used by many students and, therefore, kept in reserve either permanently or for a specified period only (for example, duration of a project for which they will be needed by all the members of specific group/class). This department may also serve to control circulation of other restricted material.

Basic requirements: counter, and possibly an office, with shelving behind to hold material. Floor area needed will depend largely on quantity of material to be housed.

Generally close to main entrance and circulation desk; must be close to suitable reading area(s).

See 2.24.4: 'Bookstacks' and 2.24.3: 'Counters and service desks'.

2.24.2 Facilities for associated activities

Children's room

Accommodation for activities sponsored by the library: story hours, table games, talks, films, puppet shows and creative play (art, model making etc.). Some of these activities may be provided for in the children's lending department (p.76) and/or in a general purpose room or small lecture hall/theatre (p.86).

If creative activities are to be included in library programme a separate space is ideal so that projects and materials need not necessarily be packed away after each session. Allow 3 m² of floor space per child and, if possible, provide at least enough space for a typical school class – 15-30 children.

Should be closely linked to children's lending department. If room is to be used outside library opening hours it must be planned to be used independently.
Consider noise generated in this space when deciding on location.
Provide sufficient storage for craft supplies, stackable chairs, tables etc.
Consider provision for display of art and craft work: pinning boards on walls, shelves etc.

Furniture and fittings: tables should preferably be small units (say 600 mm × 900 mm) which can be placed together to form larger units.
A sink with drainer, a writing board and pinning boards should be provided.
If slides and/or films are to be shown, a wall-mounted screen and blackout blinds may be required.
Floors: easy to clean; washable.
Lighting: minimum of 350 lux on working plane.
Good daylighting normally considered essential.

Meeting/seminar or general purpose rooms

Must generally accommodate a variety of activities which may include some, or all, of the following: meetings, lectures, readings, music listening, films and exhibitions. May be multi-purpose, for example, so designed that it/they could be used as extension to a reading area. Danish standards for public libraries recommend that one general purpose room be provided for each 5,000-6,000 of population served. Rooms should accommodate 15-25 people allowing approximately 2 m² of floor area per person which includes space for circulation. Extra area will need to be added for special facilities such as projection booth.

Likely to be used outside library opening hours: locate so that they can be used independently.
Consider access to lavatories and, possibly, kitchen facilities. In academic libraries seminar rooms may be required close to bookstack and reading areas.

Furniture and fittings: to ensure flexibility of use tables should be small units (say 600 mm × 900 mm) which can be placed together to form larger units. A writing board, wall-mounted projection screen, built-in speakers, platform, projection facilities and blackout blinds may be required.

Walls: may have to be suitable for exhibition purposes; rails or other system for hanging pictures should be considered.

Lighting: approximately 300 lux on table tops; 500 lux on writing board. Separate flexible spotlights on tracks may be needed for wall displays etc.

Acoustics: may be difficult to make room suitable for various functions. Specialist advice should be obtained.

Fittings: some or all of the following may have to be provided: platform/stage, writing board, wall-mounted projection screen.

Projection booth: with double-glazed window; maximum flexibility for different types of projectors (possibly on trolleys); table top for rewinding 16 mm films; shelves for reels and other equipment; lighting controlled by dimmer switch.

Consider rear screen projection: has advantage of being able to be used in lighted room.

Acoustics: consider position of absorbent surfaces: some hard surfaces may be required for resonance and overtones (for music).

Lighting: specialist advice must be obtained.

Fittings: rails or other system for hanging pictures on wall. Consult specialist manufacturers/suppliers for detailed information on exhibition display systems.

Lighting: 300 lux on display. Should be flexible system, for example, adjustable spotlights on track. Consider special requirements for permanent displays: in glass showcases etc. Specialist advice should be obtained.

Consider sub-dividing or linking rooms with movable acoustic room dividers for more flexibility of use.

At least one room may need projection facilities; also suitable equipment and good acoustical conditions for the stereophonic reproduction of music.

Provide sufficient storage for the various possible needs: stackable chairs, tables, movable platforms, audio-visual equipment etc.

Lecture hall/theatre

A space suitable for relatively large groups; it may be required to accommodate various functions: lectures, films, music recitals, amateur dramatics etc. Floor area may be roughly calculated allowing 1 m^2 per person: this would include circulation aisles but not special facilities (for example, a projection booth – which could double as a control room for sound and lighting); stage/platform (movable or permanent). Area for these must be added.

Likely to be used outside library opening hours: locate so that it can be used independently.

Consider access to lavatories and, possibly, kitchen facilities.

Changing-room(s) may be needed if space is to be used as a simple theatre at times. A large external door should be provided for bringing in piano, scenery and other equipment.

Designing for flexibility may be a problem, for example, consider: shape of space, sloping floor versus level floor, acoustical treatment etc. Provide sufficient storage for the various possible needs.

Exhibition space

This may be integrated into one or more of the main departments (for example, adult lending) or circulation areas when approximately 10 per cent of the floor area should be added.

If separate space is provided it should ideally be capable of being used for a variety of functions. If correctly planned a general purpose room or multi-purpose lecture hall (see above) could be used. Space may have to be provided for delivery, preparation and storage of exhibition material.

Should ideally be located off main entrance and visible to all library users. Consider making it visible from outside the building to attract passers-by. Determine:

—   whether exhibition space is to be used for any permanent displays.

—   requirements for security and supervision. Space should be capable of being used to accomm᷄ late different types of exhibits: paintings, sculpture, crafts etc.

2.24.3 Administrative and work areas

Counters and service desks

Size and shape of counter depends on: size and type of library; functions to be performed at counter (issue and return of loan material, enquiries, registering of new borrowers, control and supervision etc.); issue system used (card and ticket, photographic or computerised); type of exit control (manned by inspector or electronic) which may be combined with counter; storage required (for reserved books, returned books etc.) and the maximum number of staff on duty at any one time (for example, during peak periods).

In small libraries the counter is often linear – possibly with workroom behind; all the functions are usually performed from here. In medium to large libraries functions are usually dispersed and a number of counters/service desks are provided (see below). The main circulation counter may be an island type and L- or U-shaped with separate areas/positions for return and issue operations.

Separate circulation counters may be required for the adults' and children's departments. Standards for academic libraries in the UK recommend a floor area for the counter space of $0.13\,\text{m}^2$ per reader station provided.

In medium to large libraries various service points will be required: inter-library loans; issues from reserve collection; issues from closed stack areas; enquiries; subject departments etc.

Enquiry counter/desk is usually separate from circulation counter in larger libraries: in addition to bibliographic enquiries the staff may have to deal with registering of new borrowers, retrieving and returning material from closed stacks, supervision of user activities etc. In some public libraries this is expanded into an information-media counter which will also control data terminals and other audio-visual equipment.

Subject departments (as in academic libraries) may each need a reader service point. In larger public libraries service points will be needed in separate departments: reference, periodicals and newspapers, special collections, audio-visual.

Minimum requirements will be desk and chair with personal shelves for bibliographic and reference material as well as at least one chair for enquirer. Allow floor area of approximately $4\,\text{m}^2$ depending on location, for example, freestanding or against wall. For counters space requirements will depend on function, number of staff, storage and visual display required, equipment to be housed etc.

Circulation counter must be in a prominent position (it is sometimes located in the entrance – it must at least be visible from this area) with control of entrance and exit to library areas.

Determine whether all library users will be required to pass this point on entering and leaving. Separate circulation counters may be required for adults' and children's lending departments.

Circulation counter: staff work height (about 800 mm from floor) will be determined by type of issue equipment (trays for cards or computer console etc.) and staff working requirements (standing and seated on high stools or other methods).

Counter height for public: approximately 1 m for adults and 800 mm for children.

Specialist advice should be obtained on issue systems and specific space and other requirements for each.

Fig. 2.9 *Typical layouts and dimensions for circulation counters.*

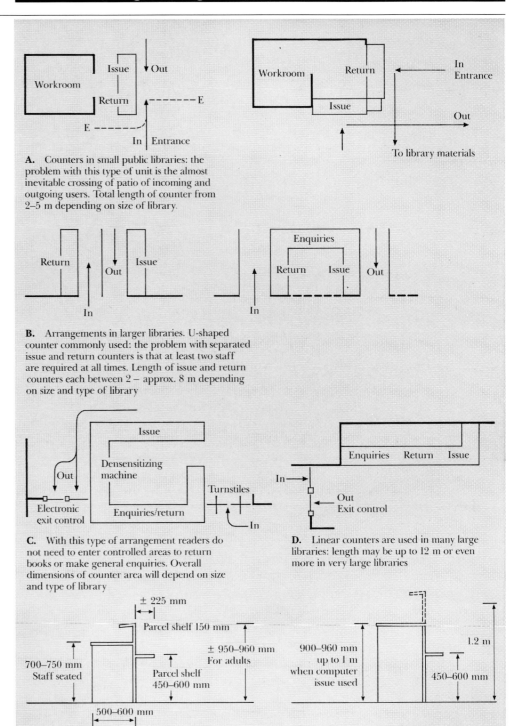

A. Counters in small public libraries: the problem with this type of unit is the almost inevitable crossing of patio of incoming and outgoing users. Total length of counter from 2–5 m depending on size of library.

B. Arrangements in larger libraries. U-shaped counter commonly used: the problem with separated issue and return counters is that at least two staff are required at all times. Length of issue and return counters each between 2 – approx. 8 m depending on size and type of library

C. With this type of arrangement readers do not need to enter controlled areas to return books or make general enquiries. Overall dimensions of counter area will depend on size and type of library

D. Linear counters are used in many large libraries: length may be up to 12 m or even more in very large libraries

E. Counter for staff seated and for children (counter on children's side also 700–750 mm)

F. Counter for staff standing or on high stools

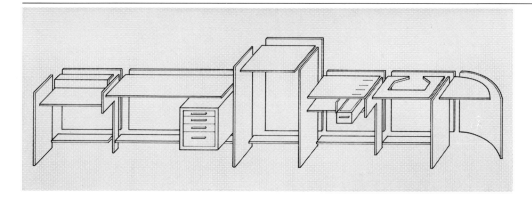

Fig. 2.10 *A typical circulation desk built up from proprietary modular elements.*

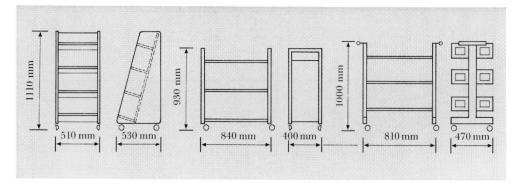

Fig. 2.11 *Book trolleys: details and dimensions vary from manufacturer to manufacturer. Illustrated left is a typical standard range.*

Determine what other counters/service desks will be required. For all of them consider:

— which need to be close to the main entrance and to the main circulation counter (for example, inter-library loan, reserve collection).

— which need to be close to the catalogue (for example, main circulation counter, enquiries or information-media, reference, inter-library loan).

— which need direct – or at least easy – access to an office or staff work space.

— whether turnstiles are required at entry points.

— whether exit control is required and if so what system will be used, e.g. manual inspection or electronically operated barrier etc. If electronic detection is used, allow counter space for desensitising machine.

— shape, design and location of counter to ensure convenient flow of traffic without crossing out routes.

— location to ensure good sight-lines for supervision of public areas.

— storage required for books, audio-visual equipment, trolleys, lost property etc.

— space requirements in front of counter for public and behind counter for staff, furniture and equipment (computer consoles, telex machine, microfilm readers etc.).

Determine which issue system will be used at circulation counter(s); what equipment will be required and how much counter space must be provided.

Counters may be commercially produced in modular components: specialist manufacturers should be approached for detailed information. See Figs 2.9, 2.10, 2.11 (also Fig.2.15).

Security: specialist advice should be obtained on the most up-to-date systems for exit control together with relevant information on space and other requirements. Security mirrors or closed circuit television may be needed to assist supervision of public areas from counter.

Telecommunications: consider position of main telephone. Counters and desks may need external and/or internal telephones. Sound reproducing equipment may be operated/controlled from one or more of the service counters.

Service outlets: consider cable and outlet positions for electronic and audio-visual equipment, e.g., computer consoles, telex, detectors, microreaders etc. Specialist advice should be obtained on the specific requirements for the various equipment to be provided for.

Lighting: 500 lux on counter. Generally localised lighting combined with general lighting over counter/service desk and working space. Switches controlling lighting may be required at (or adjacent to) main circulation counter.

Photocopying service

Requirements will vary depending on the size and type of library. In a small public library a single machine (possibly coin operated) may be placed in the entrance or one of the departments (for example, reference). Separate space, usually with service counter/desk, is generally needed in academic and large public libraries. Approximately $5\,m^2$ of floor area should be allowed for each machine.

Equipment: detailed information on space and other requirements should be obtained from manufacturers/suppliers.
Acoustics: ceiling and walls may need to be sound absorbent.

Facilities should be easily accessible from public areas, particularly periodicals and reference.

The activity and the machines generate noise; space should be located so that it will not disturb users in areas which need to be quiet.

Consider:

—   system to be used: staff or public to operate machines?
—   need for seating for users having to wait.
—   storage requirements.

Catalogue

Space requirements vary greatly according to the system used (cards in cabinets, computer printout in bookform or on microfilm, on-line computer consoles etc.), cataloguing practice, type and size of library etc. If computer consoles are used these may be placed at various points throughout the library. With card catalogues provision must generally be made for 3 cards per volume. Card trays 430 mm deep filled to about 70 per cent of capacity will take 1,000 cards. Standard cabinets may be 5 or 6 trays wide (800 mm-1 m); number of drawers per vertical row approximately 6 – there may be more if standing height tables, on which trays can be consulted, are provided adjacent to cabinets. Each metre length of one-sided catalogue will need approximately $3\,m^2$ ($6\,m^2$ if double-sided) of floor area; this includes space for catalogue users and circulation (passage space). Space for consultation tables, other catalogue forms (for example, printed volumes and computer consoles) and anticipated growth should be added.

Cabinets and other equipment: consult specialist manufacturers/suppliers for detailed information. See Figs 2.12 and 2.13.
Lighting: 150 lux vertically on card cabinet and 500 lux on consultation tables. Where rows of luminaires are used their axes should be parallel to catalogue cabinets, that is, at right angles to pulled-out drawers.

The catalogue is an important element: the key to the contents of the library. It should, therefore, be carefully located.

Consider:

—   that it should be close to the entrance, easily accessible from circulation desk and *en route* to all departments which it serves.
—   that it should be near to the collection of bibliographies and the reference/enquiries (or information) service.
—   that it should be easily accessible from inter-library loans and the technical process areas (catalogue and acquisitions departments).
—   that it is a focus of activity and should be so placed that it will not be a source of distraction to other users.
—   that the catalogue may be divided, for example, subject catalogue and author/title catalogue.

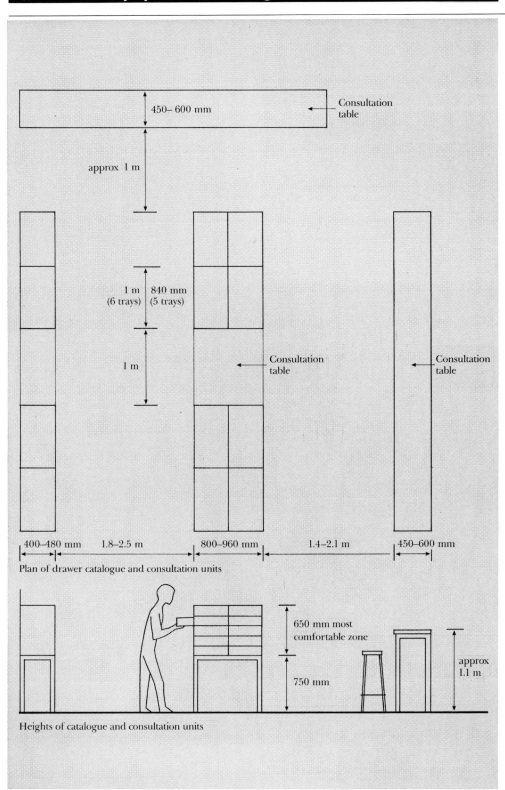

Fig. 2.12 *Typical dimensions in card catalogue area. Plan indicates alternative positions for consultation tables: tables in line with and between catalogue units may tend to obstruct adjacent drawers.*

Consultation table

450–600 mm

approx 1 m

1 m (6 trays) | 840 mm (5 trays)

1 m

Consultation table

Consultation table

400–480 mm | 1.8–2.5 m | 800–960 mm | 1.4–2.1 m | 450–600 mm

Plan of drawer catalogue and consultation units

650 mm most comfortable zone

750 mm

approx 1.1 m

Heights of catalogue and consultation units

Fig. 2.13 *Various proprietary modular card catalogue systems are available. Illustrated above are some typical elements.*

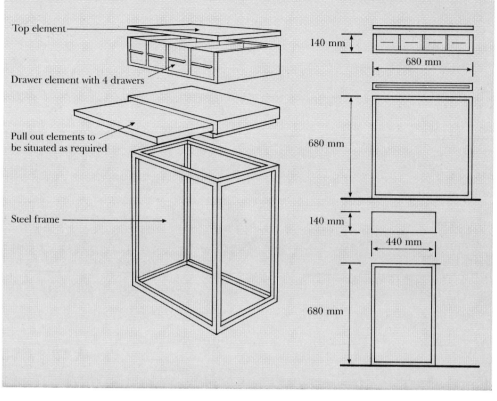

Fig. 2.14 *Dimensions for typical workstation with typing return and desk.*

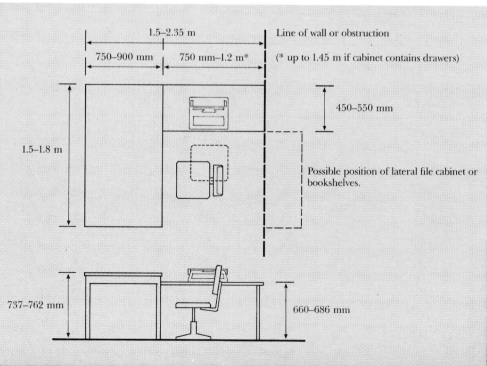

Offices and workrooms

The facilities needed will depend upon the size and type of library. A small public library may require only one space – possibly sub-divided into office and workroom – for all functions.

In larger libraries some, or all, of the following must be provided: offices for chief librarian and other senior staff; individual offices or general work areas for secretarial/clerical staff; offices for departmental librarians (reference, periodicals, lending departments) and for each of the technical process areas (workrooms); work space for dispatch and arrivals, accessioning, cataloguing and classifying, periodicals (serials), processing and, possibly, binding. Space may also be required for office/printing machines (duplicating, photocopying etc), a photographic/graphic production department, a post room and a maintenance workshop.

The IFLA suggests that there is usually a close relationship between the areas required for offices and workrooms, and those of the main public departments. It recommends that 20 per cent of the total area of public departments will be adequate for offices and workrooms: this will be equivalent to approximately 10-12 m^2 of floor area per staff member.

The chief librarian may need an office of 18-30 m^2 depending on whether it is to be used for committee meetings. Other individual offices 10-15 m^2; space per person in general offices 7-9 m^2; space per person in technical process workrooms 12-14 m^2.

Consider whether all offices are to be centralised, or alternatively, which are to be located with related public departments and technical process areas; also which need to be accessible to the public. Consider provision of waiting area for visitors. Determine which technical processes are to be in separate areas and which in a general space that can be sub-divided and rearranged freely. In both cases ensure that positioning of spaces in relation to each other corresponds to the sequence of work processes involved.

Define activities in each area and trace routes of materials from delivery to shelves, for example:

— accessioning: bibliographic checking of material recommended for purchase, preparation of orders, receiving and inspection of delivered material etc. Must be close to cataloguing and to dispatch/arrivals.

— cataloguing: to classify and catalogue material and maintain bibliographic records. Adjacent to accessioning and card production area of processing. Work requires concentration; must be adequately screened from noisy areas.

— processing: preparation of material after cataloguing and before placing on shelves: cards, labels, pockets etc – also repair of books from stack.

— periodicals (serials): to receive, record, catalogue and route to their proper location all periodicals, newspapers etc. Close to other workrooms, dispatch/arrivals and postal delivery room; as close as possible to periodicals/newspaper room.

Furniture: list all furniture needed in each of the offices and workrooms: large tables, shelving, storage units for stationery and equipment, workstation furniture etc. If open-plan type office and work areas are to be provided consider the various proprietary workstation systems available: most include a range of furniture and screens and make provision for wire management. Furniture should allow for flexibility and be as adaptable to change as possible.

Consider special requirements for electronic machines/equipment to be used. See Figs 2.14, 2.15, 2.16.

Equipment: consider what equipment will be needed in each office and workroom, for example, photographic/graphic production: cameras, light table, copiers, printers, processors, audio recorders etc.

Specialist advice should be obtained on space and other requirements. Note: most photographic equipment for microcopy work is designed to process material in daylight but a darkroom may be needed. See Fig. 2.17.

Service outlets: flexible provision for cables and outlets for electronic equipment, machines and telephones to allow for maximum possible adaptability of workstations.

Photographic/graphic production department will have special requirements. Specialist advice should be obtained.

Lighting: general offices and workrooms 500 lux on desks/work surfaces; copytyping and business machines 750 lux on desks/work surfaces. Quality of light important; care must be taken at workstations to prevent veiling reflections, particularly on screens of computer consoles etc. Specialist advice should be obtained for lighting requirements in photographic department and darkroom.

Acoustics: soundproofing of areas generating noise: typists, punch operators, telex, computer printer etc; a soundproof booth may be required in graphic production department for audio recording.

Fittings: a sink with drainer and place for a small refrigerator, a hotplate and urn should be provided in the kitchen. Lockers may be required in cloakroom(s) – ensure that they are large enough to take outdoor clothes.

Lighting: 150 lux on table in restroom and on floor in lavatories and cloakrooms.

Consider the following:
— furniture, equipment and storage space needed in each office and workroom.
— circulation of staff and materials: space for parking and moving trolleys, conveyors etc; easy access from workspaces to all departments, to the circulation counter, the stack areas and the main catalogue.
— location of noisy areas and machines.
— design of spaces that are flexible and as adaptable to change as possible.

Staff restroom, cloakroom(s) and lavatories

Floor areas required will depend on the number of staff. Allow a total of 2-4 m^2 per staff member: 2-10 staff, 4 m^2 each; 20 staff, 3 m^2 each, with progressively less until 200 staff, 2 m^2 each.

For staff restroom allow approximately 1 m^2 per staff member with a minimum area of 10-15 m^2. In large libraries two spaces may be required: one for professional and clerical staff and one for general, technical and maintenance staff. Consider small separate rest area for women, possibly located adjacent to their lavatory.

One WC and one wash-basin will be adequate for up to 15 persons. In small libraries with few staff members facilities may be shared by males and females; in medium to large libraries separate facilities should be provided.

Restroom should be located in quiet area of building close to cloakroom(s) and lavatories; access from offices and workrooms should be easy; should be on outside wall with window.

Restroom should have facilities for tea/coffee-making and for staff to prepare simple hot meals for themselves.

Decide whether toilets are to be centralised or provided on each level in a multifloor building.

Cloakroom(s) should ideally be close to staff entrance.

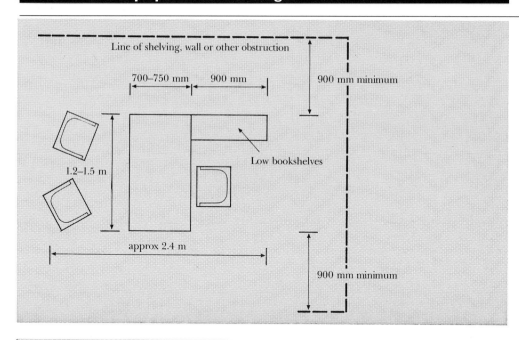

Fig. 2.15 *Dimensions for typical service point with visitor seating.*

Line of shelving, wall or other obstruction

700–750 mm   900 mm   900 mm minimum

1.2–1.5 m

Low bookshelves

approx 2.4 m

900 mm minimum

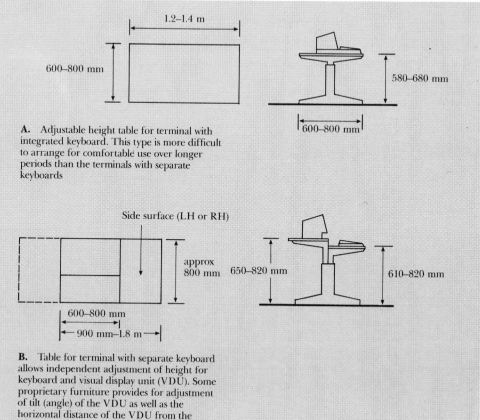

Fig. 2.16 *Typical dimensions for computer terminal tables: dimensions for proprietary units vary from manufacturer to manufacturer.*

1.2–1.4 m

600–800 mm

580–680 mm

600–800 mm

A. Adjustable height table for terminal with integrated keyboard. This type is more difficult to arrange for comfortable use over longer periods than the terminals with separate keyboards

Side surface (LH or RH)

approx 800 mm   650–820 mm   610–820 mm

600–800 mm

900 mm–1.8 m

B. Table for terminal with separate keyboard allows independent adjustment of height for keyboard and visual display unit (VDU). Some proprietary furniture provides for adjustment of tilt (angle) of the VDU as well as the horizontal distance of the VDU from the operator

Fig. 2.17 *Some typical dimensions of microreproduction equipment: dimensions of some equipment will vary greatly from manufacturer to manufacturer.*

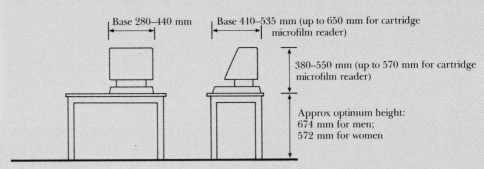

Base 280–440 mm

Base 410–535 mm (up to 650 mm for cartridge microfilm reader)

380–550 mm (up to 570 mm for cartridge microfilm reader)

Approx optimum height: 674 mm for men; 572 mm for women

A. Microfilm and microfiche readers

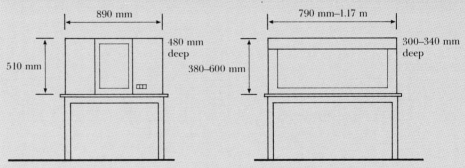

890 mm

480 mm deep

510 mm

380–600 mm

B. Kodak 'Oracle' microfilm reader printer

790 mm–1.17 m

300–340 mm deep

C. Agfa-Gevaert 'Copex' microfilm processors (daylight-type for 16 and 35 mm microfilms).

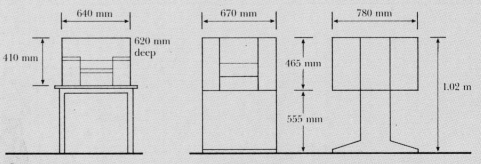
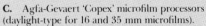

640 mm

620 mm deep

410 mm

D. Agfa-Gevaert 'Copex' desk top microfilm camera

670 mm

465 mm

555 mm

780 mm

1.02 m

E. Agfa-Gevaert 'Copex' floor type (desk model and base unit) microfilm camera

2.24.4 Materials and storage

Bookstacks – closed access

Almost all libraries need some closed stacks. There is, however, no standard for determining the amount. This will vary with the type and size of library, and the system used. Shelving units are usually 900 mm wide, 220 mm deep (up to 350 mm for oversized books) and 7 shelves high: from floor to top shelf 1.93 m and to top of unit approximately 2.3 m. A single-sided unit of these dimensions will house approximately 125 books (85 per cent capacity equals a full shelf) and 10,000 plus microcards in boxes.

Stack ranges usually in rows with an aisle of approximately 600 mm-1 m between rows: centre to centre spacing of ranges 1.05-1.5 m. As a rough guide allow 5.5 m^2 of floor area per 1,000 volumes to be housed – this includes modest provision for expansion. If compact shelving is to be used the capacity will be doubled.

Bookstacks – open access

This system is used in many academic libraries. Shelving units as for closed access but aisle between ranges about 760-1560 mm: centre to centre spacing of ranges 1.2-2 m.

As a rough guide allow 7 m^2 of floor area per 1,000 volumes to be housed – this includes modest provision for expansion; 9 m^2 of floor area per 1,000 volumes includes space for readers and reasonable expansion of the collection.

Consider position of closed access stacks in relation to public departments to be served: below them in basement; in centre of building surrounded by public areas; bookstacks behind public areas; bookstacks in form of a tower; centralised and/or local (reference, music, rare books etc separate). Location of compact storage units will be influenced by the heavy loads they impose.

Determine method of delivery between stack and public areas.

Consider system to be used in open-access plans: one room; multi-room; open plan – large areas divided by screens; subject departmentalisation etc.

In all cases layout of stack ranges must be determined (to achieve optimum centre-to-centre spacing and aisle widths so that there is adequate space for book trolleys; also determine position and width of cross aisle etc) in relation to structural grid (see p.99).

In open-access plans consider layout of stack ranges in relation to the various forms of seating, seminar rooms and staff service counters/desks.

Layout of ranges must allow for simple and logical arrangement of material with clear and continuous sequence so that there are minimum interruptions and changes of direction. Limit length of ranges to between 5.4-9 m (may be longer in closed access).

Shelving: should ideally be adjustable in vertical direction. Two basic construction types: continuous uprights (closed type) usually of same width as shelves, and bracket systems (open type). Consider:

– choice of material: wood or metal, or a combination, for example, metal frame/supports and wood shelves or steel units with wood end panels and/or wood canopies (or fascias).

– reading tables and/or pull-out reference shelves as part of the units.

– provision for lettering on front edge of shelves and canopies (or fascias) and shelf-mounted sliding book supports.

A variety of proprietary units is available and detailed information should be obtained from manufacturers/suppliers. This also applies to compact storage systems which may be either hand- or motor-operated.

Lighting: 150 lux vertically at floor level. Consider:

– type: integrated or canopy with flexible power supply to allow freedom to alter stack spacing or layout; or overhead fluorescent luminaires in continuous rows running either parallel or at right angles to bookshelves (the latter allows greater flexibility of stack spacing).

– suitability for reading in open-access system.

– light-coloured floor to increase illuminance on lower shelves.

Floor to ceiling height: about 2.3 m when lighting parallel to stacks; 2.6 m when at right angles (2.7-2.8 m if fire sprinklers are used). See Fig.2.18.

Fig. 2.18 *Bookstacks: aisle widths and lighting.*

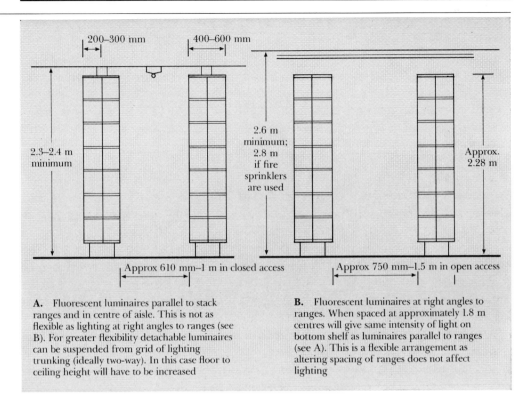

A. Fluorescent luminaires parallel to stack ranges and in centre of aisle. This is not as flexible as lighting at right angles to ranges (see B). For greater flexibility detachable luminaires can be suspended from grid of lighting trunking (ideally two-way). In this case floor to ceiling height will have to be increased

B. Fluorescent luminaires at right angles to ranges. When spaced at approximately 1.8 m centres will give same intensity of light on bottom shelf as luminaires parallel to ranges (see A). This is a flexible arrangement as altering spacing of ranges does not affect lighting

Storage units: should be non-combustible, permit free circulation of air (for example, metal filing cabinets should have louvred openings) and have easily adjustable shelves.

Environmental conditions: careful control is essential and expert advice should be obtained. A separate air-conditioning unit for this space is advisable. Temperature should be kept constant between 13-18°C and relative humidity constant between 55-65 per cent. Incoming air should be filtered with 6 air changes per hour.

Lighting: 150 lux vertically at floor level. Fluorescent luminaires should have ultra-violet filters and fused ballasts.

Fire: very sensitive detection system and, possibly, gaseous extinguishing system.

Archive/rare books store

A room may be required for closed access storage of rare and/or valuable documents, books and other material. The area required will depend on the type and amount of material to be housed. As the format of materials, and the storage fittings required, may vary considerably it is unlikely that uniformity in layout and dimension of units can be achieved. Shelving units are generally 900 mm or 1 m wide, 350-500 mm deep and 2.3 m high. Aisles should be a minimum of 1.1 m wide and the length of ranges should not exceed 9 m.

Location: adjacent to or easily accessible from rare book reading/display room but not in basement where water may accumulate, nor directly under roof where there is a danger of water seepage. Internal location (or on north wall in northern hemisphere) will help to minimise impact of outside temperature.

Maximum protection against theft is usually required and it must be possible to supervise access to the room which should, ideally, have no windows.

Consider fire resistance (1½ hours) of enclosing walls, floor and roof/ceiling.

Audio-visual material store/stack

Audio-visual material (microforms, films, slides, records, tapes) is often accommodated in open-access units in the various public departments together with related book collections or, alternatively, in a separate specialised space. Some of the material, however, may need to be housed in a closed-access stack that is dust-free with a constant temperature and humidity. It may, therefore, be advisable, even in a large departmentalised library, to keep much of the audio-visual collection in a central store.

The area required will depend on the amount and type of material to be housed.

Location: easily accessible from all public areas/departments using the materials, and adjacent or close to audio-visual equipment store and photographic department.

Structural grid

A priority in planning a modular (or flexible) library is to determine a suitable structural grid (that is, column spacing) which will allow not only adaptability within the framework but also economical use of space.

In addition to layout and function there are various other factors which affect column spacing: height of building, materials and structural system, cost etc. One grid may not be suitable for all areas or functions. A grid is generally based on optimum spacing of shelving ranges in stack areas and on the optimum length of ranges (a multiple of length of standard shelving units – usually 900 mm or 1 m). A square grid has advantages as it allows shelving units to run in either direction. For maximum balance between cost and utility it has generally been found that the grid should be at least 6 m square and at most 8.4 m square. Although a larger spacing between columns is usually better from a functional point of view, it may be very costly. See Fig.2.19.

Consider the following:
— suitability of structural grid for seating layouts, carrels, office sub-divisions and stack layout. The grid should, as far as possible, allow for at least three possible stack centres.
— the relationship of the structural grid to the grid of services – lighting, heating, air-conditioning etc – in terms of suitability and flexibility.
— the building façade, for example, window spacing.
— the effect on adaptability of using different grids in different parts of the library.

Book circulation

In small libraries books are usually moved manually, on book trolleys. In larger libraries various mechanical handling systems may be used such as book and book-trolley lifts or book conveyors (vertical and/or horizontal). Automated book retrieval systems are also available. These systems are complicated and expensive but their cost needs to be considered against saving of space and staff. Special communications systems may be required in large libraries with closed stacks to assist the circulation of books between these areas and the service points.

The area required will depend on the system(s) used.

Furniture: detailed information on shelves, racks and cabinets for storage of audio-visual material should be obtained from specialist manufacturers/suppliers.

Environmental conditions: the air-conditioning should provide a constant temperature of between 10-16°C and relative humidity of 40-55 per cent. The air should be filtered and there should be 6 air changes per hour.

Magnetic tapes: should not be stored near magnetic fields, for example, those produced by heavy wiring installations.

Columns: should not, if possible, be larger than 450 mm × 450 mm so that they do not project beyond the shelving units into the aisles.

Fig. 2.19 *Illustration of relationship between structural grid and spacing of bookstack ranges. In closed-access stacks gangways (cross-aisles) may be provided in every other grid square rather than every square as shown. No one grid is ideal for all library functions.*

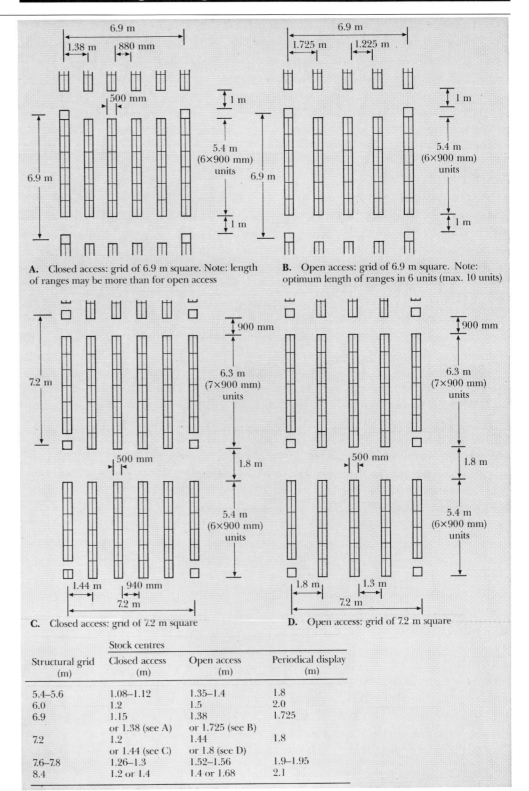

A. Closed access: grid of 6.9 m square. Note: length of ranges may be more than for open access

B. Open access: grid of 6.9 m square. Note: optimum length of ranges in 6 units (max. 10 units)

C. Closed access: grid of 7.2 m square

D. Open access: grid of 7.2 m square

Structural grid (m)	Stock centres		
	Closed access (m)	Open access (m)	Periodical display (m)
5.4–5.6	1.08–1.12	1.35–1.4	1.8
6.0	1.2	1.5	2.0
6.9	1.15 or 1.38 (see A)	1.38 or 1.725 (see B)	1.725
7.2	1.2 or 1.44 (see C)	1.44 or 1.8 (see D)	1.8
7.6–7.8	1.26–1.3	1.52–1.56	1.9–1.95
8.4	1.2 or 1.4	1.4 or 1.68	2.1

Consider the following:

— loading and off-loading of books and other materials at the arrivals/ delivery area: a ramp, platform or dock-leveller may be needed.

— type of material to be handled and flow pattern: which areas/stations need to be linked by mechanical handling systems; which require horizontal or vertical, or a combination of both.

Automated book retrieval systems will need to be located on lowest floor level because of heavy loads imposed: stacks may be 7 m or more high.

2.24.5 Ancillary spaces

Entrance hall and circulation spaces

The entrance hall must be large enough to accommodate normal flow of public and may need to include enough floor area for waiting and various other facilities: there must be sufficient space for people to look at the noticeboard, the building directory and displays of new material without causing obstruction. A draught lobby may be required.

If entrance hall is also to serve meeting and/or lecture rooms etc consideration must be given to the maximum number of people leaving these areas at any one time. The IFLA recommends that 10-15 per cent of all public areas and 20-25 per cent of all staff areas should be allowed for circulation. These figures make provision not only for entrance hall, corridors and stairwells but also for cloakrooms and lavatories; the higher figures are for large libraries with a high degree of division into separate rooms/departments.

Entrance should be easily identifiable from outside and easily accessible, particularly to the elderly and handicapped. Consider undercover provision for people waiting outside and for parking prams.

Provision must be made for all the elements to be included in the entrance: notice board(s), display case(s), building directory, public telephone, seating etc.

Consider which areas require direct access from the entrance hall, for example, circulation desk (which should be visible from entrance) and all public areas – including vertical circulation – which are not behind the control counter. Also ancillary facilities such as exhibition space, meeting-rooms, cloakroom, lavatories etc. If ancillary facilities are to be used outside library hours it must be possible to close off the library areas, preferably with one set of doors.

Cloakroom

Provision is difficult: readers do not like leaving coats and/or briefcases in unattended cloakrooms close to the entrance. Attendant cloakroom is usually impracticable (for example, in academic libraries with large numbers of students leaving at one time) and expensive. Possible solution is locking hangers or lockers.

For an unattended cloakroom with hangers or hooks at 150 mm in rows 3.6 m long

Equipment: detailed information on the systems under consideration should be obtained from manufacturers/suppliers. When deciding on system consider, amongst other things, the following:
– how quiet the equipment is in operation.
– what safeguards against damage to books and other materials are incorporated.
– how the system will affect the structure and services: establish what will be required, for example, three-phase electricity supply.

Floor: for automated book retrieval system floor must be designed to carry a uniformly distributed load of about $25 kN\, m^2$.

Special fittings: a book drop may be required for people to return books when library is closed. Outside slot should be large enough for books but not for records. Consider fire hazard.

Automatic doors may be advantageous for mothers with prams, people in wheelchairs etc.

Finishes: should be both attractive and durable; also easy to clean and maintain. Flooring must be non-slip and not show dirt; a generous area of door matting should be provided.

Acoustics: noise generated in entrance and other circulation spaces (for example, stairwells) should not be allowed to penetrate to reading/quiet areas.

Lighting: 150 lux scalar 1.2 m above floor level; corridors 100 lux scalar 1.2 m above floor level; stairs 150 lux on treads.

and circulation space of about $1 \, m^2$ at ends of rows allow approximately $0.1 \, m^2$ of floor area per person; for proprietary locking hangers allow $0.16 \, m^2$ per person. The area required for lockers will depend on the type used: full height, half height etc.

Lockers: size on plan ranges from $300 \, mm \times 300 \, mm$-$500 \, mm \times 500 \, mm$; standard height $1.7 \, m$.
Lighting: 150 lux on floor.

Location: adjacent to entrance hall. Alternative solution is to provide coat racks close to, and within view of, reading areas, but wet coats and umbrellas may present a problem.
If electronic exit control is being used, lockers for briefcases will usually not be needed.

Public lavatories
Statutory requirements will vary from place to place. The following is a general guide:
Men:
    WCs – minimum 2 (up to 200 persons), then 1 for each 100 up to 500
    urinals – minimum 2 (up to 1,000 persons)
    wash-basins – 1 for each 60 persons
Women:
    WCs – minimum 2 (up to 75 persons), then 1 for each 50
    wash-basins – 1 for each 60 persons

Fittings: must be robust and vandal-proof; care must be taken with detailing.
Finishes: hardwearing, impervious, easy to clean and vandal-proof.
Lighting: 150 lux on floor.

Location: in public library with meeting and lecture facilities, lavatories should be accessible to these areas – available for use when the library is closed – and to the public departments; should not be in too prominent a position but possible to supervise.
In large academic libraries toilets may be required on each level.
Consider special requirements for children and/or handicapped persons.

Refreshment area
Area required will depend largely on type of facility (snackbar, coffee shop etc) and on number of persons to be seated. With seating at tables for 4-6 people (self-service or table service) allow 0.9-$1.4 \, m^2$ per person.
Space may be required for a small kitchen. For information see Appendix A.1.b: *New Metric Handbook*[8], chapter 20.

Finishes: and design should help to create a warm, informal and relaxed atmosphere: heavy duty carpet tiles on floor can contribute towards this and help reduce noise level.
Lighting: about 200 lux on tables; in kitchen 500 lux on working surface.

Location: may need to be linked to the meeting/lecture facilities; adjacent to entrance hall and public toilets. Entrance direct from outdoors may be required if facility is to be open outside library hours. Areas into which refreshments may be taken must be clearly defined.

Bookshop
Area required will depend on type and quantity of material to be displayed; shop and its layout can obviously be varied to fit size and shape of space available.
Floor area of between 50-$80 \, m^2$ may be sufficient for a small bookshop including

space for office/workroom. For a rough indication of space requirements see 'Lending department – adults' (p.75).

Location: adjacent to, and with access from, entrance hall; shopfront/display facing entrance hall to attract the attention of passers-by. Entrance direct from outdoors may be required if shop is to remain open outside library hours.
Layout: counter with cash register near shop entrance for easy supervision. Allow sufficient room between shelving/display units for customers to browse.

Fittings: for dimensions of shelving and island units see 'Lending department – adults'.
Lighting: 150 lux vertically at floor level.

Storage

Storerooms and/or cupboards may be required for furniture, stationery, cleaning materials and general equipment (spare fluorescent tubes, access ladders etc).

Location: generally close to dispatch/arrivals bay; stationery store easily accessible from workrooms and offices. Stores should be kept fairly shallow: maximum about 5.5 m deep.

Fittings: cleaners' store may require sink with drainer for filling buckets etc.
Lighting: 150 lux on floor.

Plant rooms

These may be required for air-conditioning or heating and ventilation; also electrical substation. Space requirements will depend on size of library, systems used, and requirements of various authorities involved.

Spaces should be grouped together and located to minimise length of service runs. Certain spaces (for example, electrical substation) will require direct access from the outside.

Detailed information regarding equipment and requirements should be obtained from appropriate consultants and specialist manufacturers/suppliers.
Ventilation: must be adequate and care must be taken to ensure safe disposal of fumes (for example, from boiler).
Lighting: 100-150 lux on floor.

Mobile library service

If vans are to be based in library, garage(s) with loading and work area will be required. Allow approximately 35 m^2 per van (10 m × 3.5 m – dimensions will obviously depend on size and type of van used) plus space for loading dock/work area at back or on one side.
Bookstacks – for separate mobile library collection – may line wall of loading dock or be in a separate adjacent workroom.

Consider location in relation to service entrance/driveway and to the other workrooms of the library.
If loading dock is at rear of garage ensure that there is sufficient outdoor space for vans to manoeuvre and reverse into parking bays. If garage has an entrance at one end and an exit at the other – with loading dock on one side – reversing is eliminated.

Shelving: as for 'Bookstacks' (p.97).
Doors: overhead type are generally the most practical.
Loading dock: consider the height of the platform in relation to vehicle-bed height. Flush-folding dock-levellers – basically folding metal bridges between platform and vehicles – may be required.

2.25 Building design

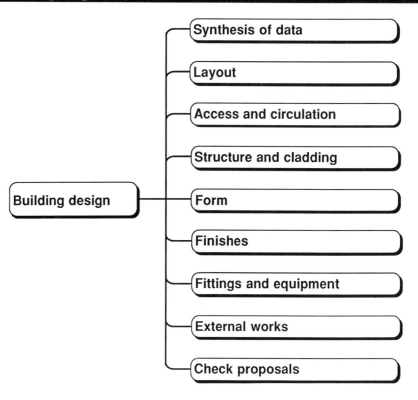

Synthesis of data
Bring together all requirements and constraints in terms of particular aspects of building design. Consider implications of all detailed data with regard to design policies and modify if required. Confirm or adjust space standards to be used for project.

Layout

See also 2.16. With new information available it may be necessary to change an idea that seemed suitable earlier on.
See 2.24.1-4 for basic information on relationships between main spaces.

Develop layout to meet site, circulation, constructional, environmental, statutory, economic and other requirements.
Consider in particular the effects of:
— phasing.
— growth and change – a design based too rigidly on specific requirements may not be satisfactory for long.
— fixed spaces (lifts, stairs, lavatories, ducts etc.) – locate in position favourable to future addition and flexibility.
— relationship to any existing, or future, adjacent building which may form part of complex, for example, in university or cultural centre.

Access and circulation

When deciding location and relationship of spaces, and patterns of circulation, consider:

— access from outside for: users, staff, goods vehicles.

— non-library facilities which must be able to operate independently.

— main and secondary control points.

— internal access to stairs and emergency exits required by fire regulations.

— internal circulation of people: users – particularly the elderly and disabled – and staff.

— internal circulation of books and other materials including need for mechanical handling (for example, conveyors).

— vertical circulation: stairs, ramps, escalators and lifts for users, staff and books; shared or separate provision.

— door widths to allow for moving of equipment and for wheelchair users – keep in mind provision of bypass for control turnstiles.

See Appendix A.1.b: *New Metric Handbook*[8], chapter 16 for general information.

Remember that the library must be not only easy to find but also easy to enter and use. Public libraries must advertise their existence – underused they are a poor investment.

If large numbers of people need to be moved vertically between one or two levels only, escalators may provide a good solution.

Structure and cladding

Develop and integrate structural proposals in light of layout. When assessing structure and cladding consider:

— structural grid (column spacing) in terms not only of optimum spacing of shelving ranges, office subdivisions, seating layouts, but also of cost, height of building, structural system etc.

— live load factors for various parts of the building. If maximum planning flexibility is required, this may involve design of entire structure to maximum live load capacity.

— sizes of internal columns – these may affect layout and flexibility of bookshelf arrangements.

— permanent loadbearing internal walls versus movable partitions.

— thermal performance: minimum heat transfer, cost-effective insulation etc. Avoid cold bridges and potential air leaks.

— risk of overheating and condensation.

— services integration – routes of elements (horizontal ducts, pneumatic tube system etc) which can seriously affect structure.

See 2.24.3. For more detailed information on column spacings in bookstacks see Appendix A.1.a: Thompson[2], chapter 8; and on structural systems see Cardin[16]. For general information see Appendix A.1.b: *AJ Handbook of Building Structure*[17] and *AJ Handbook of Building Enclosure*[18]. For information on energy conservation by the design of building fabric see Gage[19] and Markus[20].

Floor loads generally about $6.2kN/m^2$ for normal shelving (as in lending department) and $7.2kN/m^2$ for stack areas.

For compact/mobile shelving loading may be between 10.8-$16.8kN/m^2$. This type of shelving is normally located in a special permanent area – ground floor or basement the most economic position.

Form

Develop form of building in light of layout, structural and environmental aspects. Consider in particular:

— compactness: atriums or courtyards can greatly lengthen circulation distances.

— extendability: avoid towers or other forms that are difficult to extend.

See also 2.16.

Finishes

When selecting internal finishes consider:

— robustness, ease of cleaning and minimum maintenance.

— colour and surface reflectance (glare and excessive brightness contrasts

See detail/technical information 2.24.1-4.

must be avoided).

— safety, for example, non-slip floors.

— noise, for example, sound-absorbent ceilings and floors.

— appearance and effect on general environment which should be light and pleasant.

— cost: initial and long term.

Fittings and equipment

Collect information on any equipment specifically requested by client for inclusion in building and assess suitability. Determine position (in relation to circulation patterns), type and fixing of all fittings and equipment.
Consider:

— bookshelves and other storage and display units.

— reading areas: tables, chairs, carrels; also surface finishes of worktops should be matt to reduce reflected glare.

— catalogue cabinets, circulation counter, control desks.

— staff workstations: special units may be required for visual display or teletype equipment.

— what furniture will be ready-made and what will be custom-designed.

— security and control: electronic exit system, entrance turnstiles etc.

— vandalism (for example, in public lavatories if provided): components and their fixings must be robust and not invite interference.

— material handling equipment: conveyor, pneumatic tube.

— internal signage: to be flexible.

External works

Develop landscape and siting proposals in light of building design proposals, statutory requirements, and other factors.
Consider:

— access: roadways, pathways and links to adjacent or adjoining buildings.

— planting and other landscape features.

— parking areas; bicycle racks.

— outdoor lighting and external signs (directional and identifying).

— outdoor displays: vandal-proof and weatherproof.

Check proposals

Check that all objectives, resources, constraints, risks and implications of user and other requirements have been taken into consideration in the overall design.
Consider all possible conflicts, trade-offs and balances, for example:

— layout in terms of openness versus security and staffing *and* internal environmental control.

— flexibility versus form (for example, compactness) and cost of structure and services; also in terms of spatial uniformity, keeping needs of users in mind.

— economic requirements for bookstacks versus comfort of readers in terms of ceiling heights, ventilation etc.

— floor areas against original estimates.

Actual examples of all standard (ready-made) furniture and equipment being considered for the library should be seen – and competing proprietary models compared – before a final choice is made.
In the UK fittings and equipment may be seen at, or advice/information obtained from, the Library Equipment Centre at the College of Librarianship, Wales. See Appendix A.1.e. See also Appendix A.1.a: Thompson[2] and A.1.b: Ellsworth[3] for detail information.

For car parking allow 20-30 m² per space; for pedal and motor cycles 1.5 m² per space.
For detailed information see Appendix A.1.b: *New Metric Handbook*[8], chapters 7 and 40.

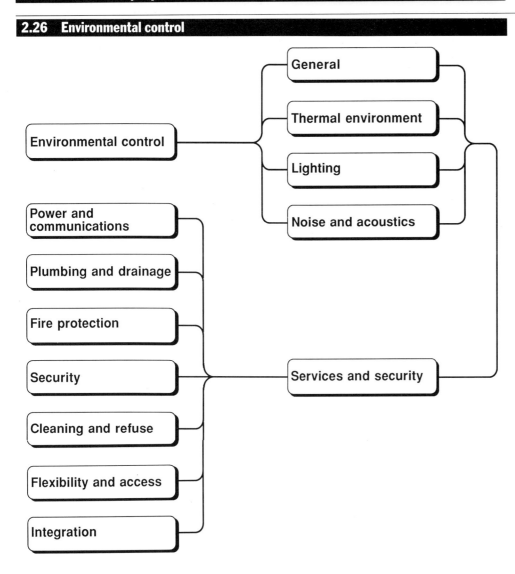

General

Develop and integrate environmental installation proposals to meet layout, constructional, statutory and economic requirements. Consider installation as a whole and no one aspect in isolation.

Close co-operation between all members of the design team is particularly important. See Appendix A.1.b: Gage[19] and Markus[20].

Thermal environment

Determine best and most economical method of ensuring fairly constant temperature and humidity levels; also of ensuring that an adequate circulation of air, free of dust and impurities, is maintained.
Consider:

Climate, amongst other things, will influence requirements which should, generally speaking, be as follows:

– in open access and staff areas constant temperatures of about 21°C (± 2°) and relative humidity between 45-55 per cent. Temperatures in closed stack areas preferably lower: between 13-18°C, but with maximum of 8°C differential to open access and staff areas; relative humidity 50-55 per cent.

– air changes per hour: 3-6 throughout year with air-conditioning, and in winter with mechanical ventilation; up to 8 per hour in summer with mechanical ventilation.

For detailed information on air-conditioning systems to minimise energy consumption see Appendix A.1.b: Sherratt[21]; for general information on heating and air-conditioning see Kell[22] and *New Metric Handbook*[8], chapter 41.

Certain areas, for example, rare bookstacks, may require air-conditioning unit separate from main system to provide the required level of filtration etc.

For approximate levels of lighting required in each of the library areas see 2.24. 1-4. For detailed information see Appendix A.1.b: *CIBS Lighting Guide: Libraries*[23]; also *New Metric Handbook*[8], chapter 43, Thompson[2], chapter 15 and Ellsworth[3], chapter 8.

Discuss emergency lighting requirements with local fire officer.

Note: great care must be taken with roof lighting. This has caused overheating in summer in many library buildings.

The quality of light (quantity/level of light; control of glare both direct and indirect; shadows) is very important: great care must be taken in selecting luminaires and lenses and in deciding on their positions. Consider having mock-ups made with fittings at correct height to test and compare all luminaires and lenses under consideration for the building. Also compare fluorescent units for noise: ballasts may have to be specially selected to ensure that hum is reduced to a minimum. Ultra-violet filters may be required on fluorescent luminaires – also fused ballasts – in certain spaces (for example, rare book areas).

— full air-conditioning most satisfactory; essential for rare/valuable material. Consider feasibility of using heat pump.

— mechanical ventilation if air-conditioning not feasible (for example, on financial grounds); consider heating and/or filtering air, and heat recovery.

— zoning of building for air-conditioning or warm-air systems.

— extracting air through air-handling luminaires.

— natural ventilation: may be difficult to achieve; will influence building form.

— position of air outlets to ensure that there is no draught on readers.

— heating: radiators and convectors will use valuable wall space: consider under-floor heating (electric or hot-water). Is district heating available?

Establish detailed requirements for plant rooms. Consider:

— location of plant to minimise distribution losses.

— access for maintenance.

— sound insulation.

Lighting

Establish lighting requirement for each of the library areas. Consider:

— what visual tasks must be provided for.

— the shape of each space in relation to sizes and position of windows etc.

— levels of lighting required overall (visual environment) and for tasks.

— natural lighting: orientation, shape and sizes of glazed areas to avoid glare, uneven light, sunlight on books, reflections and unwanted solar gain and heat loss.

— artificial lighting: appropriate system, for example, general (luminous ceiling, indirect, direct diffused), localised, task or combination; intensity, quality of light (glare, excessive contrasts), efficiency, length of life, initial and on-going costs.

— type of lamps and luminaires; also location and arrangement.

— flexibility, for example, individually controlled task lighting versus general lighting; alternatively, track with movable fittings or modular luminaires in suspended ceiling.

— veiling reflections (bright reflections in the task): particular care must be taken with visual display unit screens – lighting for these will require special consideration (an indirect lighting system).

— emergency lighting requirements: generator or batteries; automatic changeover device; separate circuit to light strategic routes and exits.

— means of access to luminaires for maintenance and cleaning.

— controls and switching patterns: control from central point, time control etc; also individual switches for rows of lights in bookstack; special switch for groups of lights for cleaners or other users out of hours.

Noise and acoustics

Ensure that the following factors have been considered:

— siting (external sources of noise).

— layout of building to minimise nuisance from noisy areas and equipment; main traffic/circulation routes away from quiet areas.

— insulation of reading and other quiet areas from necessary internal and unavoidable external noise.

— sound reduction value of external walls (generally not less than 50 dB); also fenestration – double glazing may be required.

— finishes: absorbent ceilings; flooring to reduce impact noises.

— requirements for specialised spaces: theatre, rooms for music etc.

Acceptable maximum levels of background noise are roughly:
– quiet areas – 30-35 dB
– low noise areas (staff areas; circulation counters etc) – 45-50 dB
– noisy areas (lobbies, stairs etc) – 50-60 dB
For general data on sound see Appendix A.1.b: *New Metric Handbook*[8], chapter 44.

2.27 Services and security

Power and communications

Consider:

— realistic sizes for vertical and horizontal ducts; also extent and method of providing flexibility, for example, outlets (power and communications) installed where needed on trunking (perimeter, floor or ceiling).

— power points in all spaces for: audio-visual equipment; electronic and other special equipment; floor cleaning and polishing machines etc.

— multicore cable installation and outlets for computer consoles, closed-circuit television etc.

— telephone system: one or more exchange lines each connected to a telephone instrument; or small switching systems (Keymasters); or switchboard (PMBX or PABX).

— other communication systems linked to telephone network: computer terminal via modem, facsimile transmission etc.

— special requirements for: video recording and transmission; audio-visual control room; projection room; electronic exit control etc.

— outlet points for staff and public telephones; internal telephone system; tube transmission system; teleprinters or closed-circuit television for internal communication, for example, between service points and closed stacks.

Establish detailed requirements for substation and distribution and meter rooms; also switchboard. Consider:

— access for maintenance.

— sound insulation.

See Appendix A.1.b: Corby[14] and *Communications*[15].
Computer and other electronic and communications technology is evolving so rapidly that specialist advice should be obtained at an early stage.

Plumbing and drainage

Determine requirements for hot and cold water, and drainage installations. Consider:

— position and size of ducts.

— position and space for water tank.

— method of heating water: low-pressure hot water system served from central boiler or storage cylinder with immersion heater etc.

— requirements for boiler room (if needed); also access for maintenance.

— water supply for fire sprinklers and/or hosereels.

Fire protection

Establish requirements in terms of national legislation and local by-laws, for example:

— fire-resistance of walls and doors.

— limits of floor area, height and capacity of fire compartments.

— means of escape for occupants.

Consider the following precautionary measures:

— dividing main stack areas into fire-resisting compartments (maximum of 1,420 m)^3.

— enclosing vertical openings (stairwells etc) with fire-resistant materials.

— automatic fire dampers in ducts at all points where they pass through walls and floors.

— smoke exhaust/extraction system.

— minimise use of combustible equipment: use steel fittings/furniture rather than wood.

— detector system: sensors actuated by heat, rapid rise in temperature or presence of smoke.

— extinguishers: automatic sprinkler system, for example, water (wet or dry pipe) or gaseous (for special areas: rare books, computer room etc.); portable extinguishers for dealing with outbreaks locally.

— alarms: connected to automatic detector system and central indicator panel; also, possible direct link to local fire station.

Fire precautions should be discussed with the local fire authority and fire insurers. Although various sources claim that sprinklers should not be installed as they can do more harm than good (water damage greater than damage by fire) evidence would not seem to support this argument. See Appendix A.1.b: Morris[24]. For general information see *Thinking About Fire*[12].

Detectors are generally mounted on ceiling: approximately one to each 35 m^2.

Security

Ascertain requirements for protection of building from possible break-in.

Consider:

— overall objectives: what system is required to do; what areas need special protection etc.

— forms of detectors: perimeter (on windows and doors); volumetric or acoustic devices etc.

— type of alarm: audible or silent (signalling control centre of alarm company or police) or combination (micro-processor programmed to respond in various ways).

— special storage/protection for valuable items.

— security lighting.

— problem of cleaners moving through building and/or other activities outside library hours.

Specialist advice should be obtained at an early stage.

For detailed information see Appendix A.1.b: *Security in Buildings*[13].

Cleaning and refuse

Establish how cleaning will be done and at what times; amount of refuse that accumulates weekly and method and frequency of disposal.
Consider:
— installation of central vacuum-cleaning system and rubbish chutes.
— special provision for storage of cleaning material, cleaning equipment and refuse bins.

Flexibility and access

Consider flexibility of services arrangement and ease of access for maintenance, inspection and modification.

Integration

Consider integration of the services plant and distribution spaces into the structure.

2.28   Completion of phase

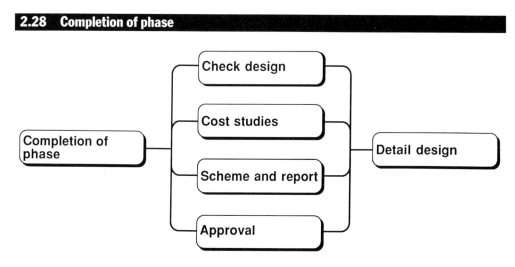

Check design

Check design proposal against recorded requirements:
— can all facilities required by client in fact be accommodated?
— confirm that all statutory requirements have been taken into account and verify that proposal meets with approval of all relevant bodies.

Cost studies

Make detailed cost estimates of building and services installation, site work etc. Also estimates of running costs, particularly those affected by design proposals, for example, staffing, maintenance, heating and cooling.
Verify that proposed design can be built within budget: modify if required.

Scheme and report

Present comprehensive proposal to client in clear and concise format:

—   drawings, models, sketches.
—   independent reports from each consultant with reasons for recommendations and appropriate analytical evidence for the selection of particular proposals.
—   cost analysis.

Approval

Note: any changes to the basic design after this point will cause delay and cost money.

Obtain client's approval before proceeding to detail design.

2.29   Detail design

See Appendix A.1.a: 'Plan of Work', Stage E in *Architect's Job Book*; and Green.

This guide is not continued beyond the phase outlined in 2.28: by that phase all major factors in the project should have been considered. This phase is concerned with completing the scheme in increasing depth of detail, something that is common to all projects.

APPENDICES

A.1 References and sources of information

a. References: section 1

1 Jones, J. Christopher, *Design Methods: Seeds of human futures*, Chichester: Wiley, 1981.

2 Palmer, M. A., *The Architect's Guide to Facility Programming*, Washington: American Institute of Architects, 1981.

3 Preiser, W.(ed.), *Facility Programming: methods and applications*, Stroudsburg, Pa.: Dowden, Hutchinson & Ross, 1978.

4 Sanoff, H., *Methods of Architectural Programming*, Stroudsburg, Pa.: Dowden, Hutchinson & Ross, 1977.

5 Alexander, C. *et al.*, *A Pattern Language: Towns, Buildings, Construction*, New York: Oxford University Press, 1977.

6a Elder, A. J., *Guide to the Building Regulations 1985* (8th edition), London: The Architectural Press, 1986. To be read in conjunction with:

6b Elder, A. J., *Guide to the Second Amendment 1981*, London: The Architectural Press, 1982.

7 Speaight, A. & Stone, G., *The AJ Legal Handbook* (3rd edition), London: The Architectural Press, 1982.

8 Mazria, E., *The Passive Solar Energy Book:* (Expanded professional edition), Emmaus, Pa: Rodale Press, 1979.

9 Koenigsberger, O. H. *et al.*, *Manual of Tropical Housing and Building*, Part 1: Climatic Design, London: Longman, 1973.

Other useful general references:

An Introduction to Cost Planning, London: The Royal Institution of Chartered Surveyors, 1976.

Architect's Job Book, compiled by L. Beaven and D. Dry (4th edition), London: RIBA Publications, 1983.

Bathurst, P. E. & Butler, D. A., *Building Cost Control Techniques* (2nd edition), London: Heinemann, 1980.

Cartlidge, D. P. & Mehrtens, I. N., *Practical Cost Planning*, London: Hutchinson, 1982.

Cross, N. & Roy, R., *Design Methods Manual* (*Man-made Futures:* Units 13-16), Milton Keynes: The Open University, 1975.

Ferry, D. J., *Cost Planning of Buildings* (4th edition revised by T. Brandon), London: Granada, 1980.

Green, R. *The Architect's Guide to Running a Job* (Amended edition), London: The Architectural Press, 1980.

Kemper, A. M., *Architectural Handbook: environmental analysis, architectural programming, design and technology, and construction*, New York: Wiley, 1979.

Lacy, R. E., *Climate and Building in Britain*, London: HMSO, 1978.

Longmore, J., *BRS Daylight Protractors*, London: HMSO, 1968.

Lynch, K., *Site Planning* (2nd edition), Cambridge, Mass.: MIT Press, 1971.

Powell, J. (ed.), *Handbook of Architectural Practice and Management* (4th edition), London: RIBA Publications, 1980.

Seeley, I. H., *Building Economics: appraisal and control of building costs and efficiency* (2nd edition), London: Macmillan, 1976.

Stone, P. A., *Building Design Evaluation: costs in use* (3rd edition), London: Spon, 1980.

b.   References: section 2

1   *Standards for Public Libraries*. IFLA Publication 9 (2nd edition), Munich: Verlag Dokumentation, 1977.

2   Thompson, G., *Planning and Design of Library Buildings* (2nd edition), London: The Architectural Press, 1977.

3   Ellsworth, R. E., *Academic Library Buildings: A Guide to Architectural Issues and Solutions*, Boulder, Colorado: The Colorado Associated University Press, 1973.

4   Ellsworth, R. E., *Planning Manual for Academic Library Buildings*, Metuchen, N. J.: Scarecrow Press, 1973.

5   *Designing a Medium-sized Public Library*, Department of Education and Science (DES), London: HMSO, 1981.

6   Withers, F. N., *Standards for Library Service*, Paris: UNESCO, 1970.

7   Brawne, M., *Libraries: architecture and equipment*, London: Pall Mall, 1970.

8   Tutt, P. & Adler, D. (eds.), *New Metric Handbook*, London: The Architectural Press, 1979.

9   Lawson, F., *Principles of Catering Design* (2nd edition), London: The Architectural Press, 1978.

10   'Energy Primer', *The Architects' Journal*, vol. 175, 19 May, 26 May and 9 June 1982.

11   Goldsmith, S., *Designing for the Disabled* (3rd edition), London: RIBA Publications, 1976.

12   'Thinking About Fire', *The Architects' Journal*, vol. 176, 11 August, 18 August and 8 September 1982.

13 'Security in Buildings', *The Architects' Journal*, vol. 171, 28 May 1980 *et seq.*

14 Corby, M., Donohue, E. J. & Hamer, M., *Telecomms Users' Handbook*, London: Telecommunications Press, 1982.

15 'Communications', *The Architects' Journal*, vol. 176, 4 August 1982.

16 Carolin, P. & Long, M. J., 'Libraries' (AD briefing series), *Architectural Design*, vol. XLIV, 7/1974.

17 Hodgkinson, A., *AJ Handbook of Building Structure* (2nd edition), London: The Architectural Press, 1980.

18 Vandenberg, M. & Elder, A. J. (eds.), *AJ Handbook of Building Enclosure*, London: The Architectural Press, 1974.

19 Gage, M. & Murphy, I., *Design and Detailing for Energy Conservation*, London: The Architectural Press, 1982.

20 Markus, T. A. & Morris, E. N., *Buildings, Climate and Energy*, London: Pitman, 1980.

21 Sherratt, A. F. C. (ed.), *Air Conditioning and Energy Conservation*, London: The Architectural Press, 1980.

22 Kell, J. R. & Martin, P. L., *Faber and Kell's Heating and Air Conditioning of Buildings* (6th edition), London: The Architectural Press, 1979.

23 CIBS Lighting Guide: *Libraries*, London: The Chartered Institution of Building Services, 1982.

24 Morris, J., *Managing the Library Fire Risk* (2nd edition), Berkeley Ca.: University of California, 1979.

Other useful references:

Cohen, A. & E., *Designing and Space Planning for Libraries*, New York: Bowker, 1979.

Lushington, N. & Mills, N. Jr., *Libraries Designed for Users*, New York: Gaylord, 1979.

Mason, E., *Mason on Library Buildings*, Metuchen, N.J.: Scarecrow Press, 1980.

Metcalf, K. D., *Planning Academic and Research Library Buildings*, New York: McGraw Hill, 1965.

Orr, J. M., *Designing Library Buildings for Activity*, London: Andre Deutsch, 1972.

Schell, H. B. (ed.), *Reader on Library Buildings*, Engelwood, Colo.: Microcard Editions Books, 1975.

c. Sources of information (general): UK

Ordnance Survey
Romsey Road
Maybush
Southampton SO9 4DH
Tel. 0703-775555
The central survey and mapping organisation in the public sector. Produces and maintains up-to-date basic surveys at 1:1,250 for major urban areas, and at 1:2,500 (minor towns and cultivated areas) or 1:10,000 (mountain and moorland) for the remainder of the country; also a range of special maps and services. Catalogues

and various leaflets are available from address given; maps obtainable through booksellers and OS agents.

The need to reproduce OS publications in whole or part is provided for by a scale of royalty charges and a series of licences designed to meet the needs of various authorities, organisations and the professions. Full information is given in OS leaflets No. 8 and No. 23.

Institute of Geological Sciences
Geological Museum
Exhibition Road
South Kensington
London SW7 2DE
Tel. 01-589 3444
also
Murchison House
West Mains Road
Edinburgh EH9 3LA
Tel. 031-667 1000

Geological survey maps are available at a scale of 1:63,360 (1 in.) (when reprinted these sheets are generally being replaced by sheets at 1:50,000, new sheets are published at 1:50,000 only) with special areas available at 1:25,000 and 1:10,560 (6 in.). Memoirs describing the geology, including details of sections, bore holes and other data have been published for many of the sheets. A catalogue of maps is available from the Institute who provide advisory services on a wide range of economic and environmental topics.

The museum contains a collection of building stones from most quarries now working stone in the UK, as well as marbles and other ornamental stones from most countries of the world. The library contains material covering the geological sciences literature of the world and is open to members of the public for reference purposes.

Meteorological Office
London Road
Bracknell
Berkshire RG12 2SZ
Tel. 0344-20242
also:
231 Corstorphine Road
Edinburgh EH12 7BB
Tel. 031-334 9721
and:
Tyrone House
Ormeau Avenue
Belfast BT2 8HH
Tel. 0232-28457

Weather information for sites in the UK (and abroad) to help with analysis and design; also provides a range of services including CLIMEST, a quick-reply service to assist the construction industry.

Various publications available (listed in leaflet No. 12). Library is open to the public and contains material covering, amongst other things, all aspects of meteorology and climatology and a large collection of world-wide data.

Department of the Environment
Air Photographs Unit
6th Floor
Prince Consort House
Albert Embankment
London SE1 7TP

A large range of aerial photography – photographs, negatives and microfilm – and a Central Register of Air Photography which contains, amongst other things, information on the coverage and scale of commercial photography.

Copies of material are available for sale.

Department of the Environment
Map Library
5th Floor
Prince Consort House
Albert Embankment
London SE1 7TP

The map library holds an extensive collection covering many aspects of town and country planning and local government, mostly of England and Wales. Selected maps are for sale – details and prices available on application.

Aerofilms Ltd
Gate Studios
Station Road
Boreham Wood
Herts WD6 1EJ
Tel. 01-207 0666

Oblique aerial photography to order; from a library collection (covering a variety of subjects including meteorology, geology, building construction, architecture) in black and white, and colour. Free proofs submitted on request; print prices and reproduction fees supplied on request. Stereo pairs available as paper prints, 35 mm slides and overhead projector transparencies.

Office of Population Censuses and Surveys
St. Catherine's House
10 Kingsway
London WC2B 6JP
Tel. 01-242 0262

Library contains population census and vital statistics reports from most countries. Open to general public (preferably by appointment).

Building Research Establishment
1) Building Research Station
Bucknalls Lane
Garston
Watford
Herts WD2 7JR
Tel. 09273-74040
2) Fire Research Station
Borehamwood
Herts WD6 2BL
Tel. 01-953 6177
3) Princes Risborough Laboratory
Princes Risborough
Aylesbury
Bucks
Tel. 084-44 3101

also:
BRE (Scottish Laboratory)
Kelvin Road
East Kilbride
Strathclyde G75 OR2
Tel. 03552-33941
The BRS covers building design and construction, environmental design etc; the Fire Research Station is concerned with fire extinction and prevention, structural aspects of fire in buildings, means of escape etc; the Princes Risborough Laboratory deals with the use of timber, wood-based and other materials in building.
Details of advisory services and publications are available from each station.

British Services Research and Information Association
Old Bracknell Lane West
Bracknell
Berks
Tel. 0344-25071
A non-profit-making association. The provision of information and advice is one of its main functions. Membership includes consulting engineers, contractors, manufacturers and others concerned with mechanical and electrical services of buildings.

British Standards Institution
2 Park Street
London W1A 2BS
Tel. 01-629 9000
Recognised body for the preparation and promulgation of standards including performance and constructional specifications and codes of practices. Enquiry service and publications available. The library contains complete sets of British Standards as well as foreign and international standards. It is open to the general public.

Fire Protection Association
Aldermary House
Queen Street
London EC4N 1TJ
Tel. 01-248 5222
Central advisory organisation (set up by insurers) covering all aspects of fire prevention and control. Provides an information service and will give technical and general advice on fire protection both at design stage and in the maintenance of buildings. Library facilities may be used by the public (preferably by appointment). A list of publications is available.

HM Stationery Office
Atlantic House
Holborn Viaduct
London EC1P 1BN
Tel. 01-583 9876
Produces hundreds of publications each year for Parliament, Government departments, museums and other public institutions in the UK.
The most useful guides are the sectional lists. These, and all HMSO publications, can be obtained from HMSO bookshops (London, Edinburgh, Manchester, Birmingham, Cardiff, Bristol and Belfast) or from booksellers appointed as stockists.

National Association of Building Centres
26 Store Street
London WC1E 7ET
Tel. 01-637 1022
Represents all building centres in the UK and Ireland with the object of co-ordinating their functions and services. The individual centres usually have a permanent exhibition of building products and provide an enquiry/advisory service. Information on the individual centres may be obtained from the National Association.

Central Council for the Disabled (Access for the Disabled)
34 Eccleston Square
London SW1
Tel. 01-821 1871
Provides a full advisory service on the design of buildings for the disabled. A list of publications on the subject is available.

Centre on Environment for the Handicapped
126 Albert Street
London NW1 7NF
Tel. 01-267 6111
Provides an advisory and information service on the design of buildings for the handicapped and for elderly people.

d. Sources of information (general): USA

US Geological Survey (Department of the Interior)
Topographic maps and indexes: benchmark locations, level data, and tables of elevations; streamflow data; water resources; geologic maps; horizontal control data; monument location.
Topographic maps available in $7\frac{1}{2}$-minute (latitude and longitude) quadrangle size plotted to scales of 1:24,000 and 1:31,680 and in 15-minute quadrangle size plotted to a scale of 1:62,500.
Geologic map of the US to a scale of 1:2,500,000.
Geologic quadrangle maps in various scales.
Mineral resource maps are also available.
An index map identifying published maps and publication date is available free from:
Map Information Service
US Geological Survey
12201 Sunrise Valley Drive
Reston, VA 22092

State Geological Surveys or equivalent state agencies
Geologic maps of most states to a scale of 1:500,000.
Mineral resource maps.

Army Map Service (Department of the Army)
Topographic maps in $7\frac{1}{2}$-minute quadrangle size plotted to a scale of 1:25,000; in 15-minute quadrangle size plotted to a scale of 1:50,000; and in 30-minute quadrangle size plotted to a scale of 1:125,000. Maps covering larger areas are prepared on scales of 1:250,000 and 1:500,000.

US National Ocean Survey (Department of Commerce)
Topographic maps; coastline charts; topographic and hydrographic studies of inland lakes and reservoirs; benchmark locations, level data, and tables of elevations; horizontal control data; seismological studies.

Soil Conservation Service (Department of Agriculture)
Local Soil Conservation Service Offices
or
Information Division
Soil Conservation Service
Washington DC 20250
Soil surveys generally covering one county (may cover several small counties or only parts of a large one) are published for all counties except Illinois. In this state the University of Illinois Agricultural Experimental Station publishes them. Surveys usually consist of maps that show the distribution of soils in the area, description of the soils, some suggestions as to their use and management, and general information about the area. An index is available.

Bureau of the Census
Census maps containing summarised population data are available for many different types and sizes of areas, for example, county, urbanised area, metropolitan and place maps. These are all available either from the Government Printing Office or the Central Users' Service.

Sanborn Map Company Inc.
Pelham NY
Sanborn fire insurance maps: these detailed maps of street layouts, building locations etc are used by insurance companies, governmental agencies, utility companies, banks etc. Local fire insurance agents are equipped with Sanborn maps of their respective cities and towns; principal offices maintain complete nationwide files.

Bureau of Land Management
Township plots, showing land divisions, state maps, showing public land and reservations; survey progress map of the USA, showing the progress of public-land surveys.

Mississippi River Commission (Department of the Army)
Hydraulic studies and flood control information.

US Forestry Service (Department of Agriculture)
Forest reserve maps including topography and culture and vegetation classification.

US Postal Service
Rural free delivery maps by counties, showing roads, streams etc.

Local municipalities: county, city, town, village.
Street maps, zoning maps, drainage maps, horizontal and vertical control data, utility maps.

US Department of Commerce: National Technical Information Service
Provides information on Government-sponsored research in different fields. Good reference material on earthquakes from annual bulletin: 'United States Earthquakes'.

US Weather Bureau and local weather stations
Historic data on weather conditions and maps of US climatic conditions.

Superintendent of Documents
Government Printing Office
Washington DC 20402
Daily weather maps published by the National Oceanic and Atmospheric Administration's Environmental Data Service. Also soil surveys, census maps etc.

Agricultural Stabilisation Conservation Service (US Department of Agriculture):
Aerial Photography Division
Eastern Laboratory
45 French Broad Avenue
Asheville
North Carolina 28802
also:
Western Laboratory
2505 Parley's Way
Salt Lake City
Utah 84109
The ASCS has a larger coverage of aerial photographs than any other single agency in the USA. An index showing which agency holds pictures of a required area can be obtained from the Map Information Service of the US Geological Survey (see address above).

'Photogrammetric Engineering'
Magazine of the American Society of Photogrammetry
An informative guide to the organisations that provide photogrammetric aerial maps.

International Federation of Library Associations and Institutions (IFLA)
Central Secretariat:
c/o Netherlands Congress Building
POB 82128
2508 EC The Hague
Netherlands
Has a membership of 166 library associations and 748 libraries in 111 countries. Advice and information can be obtained from local member associations.
A list of publications (for example: *National Library Buildings*; *National and International Library Planning*; *Standards for Public Libraries)* is available. Also publishes a quarterly journal.

Library Association
7 Ridgmount Street
London WC1E 7AE
Tel. 01-636 7543
also:
Welsh Library Association
c/o County Library HQ
Maesincla
Caernarfon
Gwynedd
and:
Scottish Library Association
c/o School of Librarianship
Robert Gordon's Institute of Technology
St Andrew Street
Aberdeen AB1 1HG
A professional organisation to promote the better administration of libraries and improve the status of librarians. The library maintains a comprehensive collection of references on all aspects of library organisation, planning and administration; advice is available on associated problems.

The Library Administration Division
American Library Association
50 East Huron Street
Chicago
Illinois 60611
Tel. 312-944 6780
Maintains a collection of information on library buildings, for example, briefs (programmes) and plans. Material is available on inter-library loan. Also holds a list of library building consultants with a summary of the projects on which they have worked.

Department of Education and Science
Elizabeth House
39 York Road
London SE1 7PH
Tel. 01-928 9222

Promotes education generally in England and Wales. Responsible for, amongst other things, the broad allocation of resources for education and the capital programmes for the building of new schools and other institutions; works in co-operation with local education authorities. Responsibility for government relations with universities in the UK is conducted through the University Grants Committee. Also has responsibilities relating to libraries. Publishes advice on educational and library buildings.

University Grants Committee
14 Park Crescent
London W1N 4DH
Tel. 01-636 7799

A permanent body (sponsored by the DES) which assesses claims from and administers funds to the universities in the UK. Published (in 1976) report of a working party containing recommendations on the future of university library buildings which is available from HMSO: *Capital Provision for University Libraries.*

Aslib
3 Belgrave Square
London SW1X 8PL
Tel. 01-235 5050

An association to promote the effective management and use of information resource in industry and commerce, central and local government, education and the professions. Offers members a comprehensive enquiry service designed to provide information on any subject. A consultancy service (on, amongst other things, the planning of special libraries) is available to members and non-members. Various publications. A list is available on application.

Educational Facilities Laboratory
477 Madison Avenue
New York
NY 10022

A source of information about new problems in library buildings, especially those involving the use of non-book media. Can advise on consultants for most aspects of library design.

Institute of Information Scientists
Harvest House
62 London Road
Reading
Berks RG1 5AJ
Tel. 0734-861 345
Particularly concerned with methods of collection, storage and retrieval of information.

The Library Equipment Centre
College of Librarianship Wales
Llanbadarn Fawr
Aberystwyth
Dyfed SY23 3AS
Tel. 0970-3181
A permanent, though changing, exhibition of library furniture and equipment with all main suppliers active in UK represented. Offers unique opportunity for librarians and architects to examine a wide range of competing equipment side by side.

In addition, the college is a rich source of information for anyone concerned with designing and planning libraries. It holds:

1) a large general collection of material on librarianship/information science including everything published in English, as well as much foreign material, on library design (books, periodical articles and audio-visual items);

2) a separate library planning collection of items on individual (or groups of) libraries. Mainly non-published materials (architects' plans and drawings, photographs, slides, descriptive brochures etc) plus copies of published articles on about 1,200 libraries throughout the world;

3) a trade literature collection with brochures, catalogues and price lists from over 600 manufacturers and suppliers.

A list of exhibitors and exhibits – updated regularly – is available for a small charge; also information on other publications from the CLW. The college has a full programme of short courses, some of which deal with aspects of library planning and design. Information is available from the Director of Short Courses at the address given above.

A.2 Site survey/ analysis

Natural factors

A. Geology and soil

Data required:

(a) Underlying geology, rock character and depth.

(b) Soil type and depth: determine value as an engineering material (for example, safe bearing capacity) and as plant medium; also suitability for septic tanks, excavation, corrosion and frost heave potential; shrink/swell characteristics.

(c) Check drainage characteristics and for signs of fill, slides and subsidence.

(d) Possible use as a building material: adobe, brick, stone.

Limitations/danger signals:

— Swelling clay or peat.

— High salt content in soil.

— Signs of past landslides.

— Evidence of creep (slippage).

— Known earthquake faults.

— Volcanic areas.

— Underlayers of impermeable materials.

— Signs of erosion.

— Rock lying close to surface.

— Made up ground (filling) or undermining.

Materials, processes, sources:
Soil survey maps and reports; geologic maps; aerial photographs. See Appendix A.1.c:
ERTS (Earth Resources Technology Satellite) images.
Trial holes (either dug pits or boreholes) with visual and tactile identification and/or laboratory testing of soil samples.
Building surveyor of local authority (UK).
Report from a geologist.

B. Topography

Data required:

(a) Height above sea level and geographical north point.

(b) Pattern of land forms.

(c) Contours, bench marks.

(d) Slope analysis, for example, orientation.

Materials, processes, sources:
ERTS images.
Topographical maps (useful for preliminary reconnaissance). See Appendix A.1.c.
Geologic maps.
Aerial photographs: preferably in stereo pairs so that site can be viewed three-dimensionally.

Site survey by architect or land surveyor.
Computer-drawn illustrations can be useful to communicate the visual feeling of a land area.

(e) Visibility analysis.
(f) Circulation analysis.
(g) Unique features.

Limitations/danger signals:

— Steep slopes (over 15 per cent).
— Undesirable slopes: west orientation, or slopes which block sun. Small buildable area. Possible problem of affecting sun-rights on adjacent properties.

C. Hydrology

Materials, processes, sources:
Geologic maps.
Aerial photographs (infra-red is best for distinguishing between land and water).
ERTS images.
Local hydrological studies.
Trial holes (either dug pits at least 2 m deep or boreholes) dug during wet season.
Local health department for testing of water samples.
Visual inspection of existing structures.

Data required:

(a) Existing water bodies: fluctuation and purity; flood levels.
(b) Natural and man-made drainage channels: flow, capacity, purity.
(c) Surface drainage pattern: amount, blockage, undrained depressions.
(d) Water table: elevation and fluctuation, springs.
(e) Underground water supply: quantity and quality.
(f) Potential for catching and storing surface water run-off in surface holding basin or underground tanks. Watersheds.

Limitations/danger signals:

— High water table.
— Underground stream.
— Undrained areas: waterlogging.
— Site or portion of site located in flood plain (below known flood level).
— Streams or water bodies polluted by sewage or industrial waste.

D. Vegetation/ecology

Materials, processes, sources:
Report from a landscape architect; ecological survey.
Aerial photographs (infra-red is valuable for distinguishing between different types of vegetation and identifying areas of plant disease).
Geologic and topographic maps.
ERTS images.

Data required:

(a) Dominant plant/animal communities: location and relative stability.
(b) Their dependence on existing factors, self-regulation and sensitivity to change.
(c) Mapping of general plant cover, including wooded areas.
(d) Specimen trees to be retained: their location, species, height and spread, and diameter at base.

Limitations/danger signals:

— Unique landscapes or those with fragile quality.
— Rare or unique flora or fauna.
— Habitat for wildlife or breeding ground.
— Migratory rest stops.
— Presence of insects (for example, mosquitoes, termites) or rodent breeding places.
— Poisonous reptiles and plants.

E. Climate

Data required:

(a) Regional data on:

— monthly mean maximum and minimum temperatures.

— monthly mean maximum and minimum relative humidities.

— total average precipitation for each month; maximum rainfall for any 24-hour period; likelihood of driving rain and intensity.

— direction and force of prevailing winds; seasonal changes.

— sky conditions; cloudiness.

— average daily amounts of solar radiation for each month; sun angles – path of daily and seasonal sun.

— average annual and monthly snowfalls.

(b) Local microclimates: warm and cool slopes, air drainage, wind deflection and local breezes, shade, heat reflection and storage, plant indications.

(c) Noise levels, smell, atmospheric quality.

(d) Regional hazards: hail, tornadoes, lightning, sand and dust storms.

Limitations/danger signals:

— Lack of vegetation.

— Severe conditions (extreme heat or cold, strong winds, severe frost).

— Site situated in natural hazard belt.

— Odours, smoke and dust from industrial or other sources.

— Noise and vibration from traffic or trains; industrial or recreational sources etc.

— Cold pockets in low-lying areas.

— Excessively windy, for example, crest of hill.

— Cold winter winds and wind funnels.

F. Natural amenities

Data required:

(a) Character of visual spaces.

(b) Viewpoints, vistas.

(c) Quality and variation of light, sound, smell, feel.

Limitations/danger signals:

— Undesirable views or unpleasant character of one kind or another: barren, bleak, depressing, dirty, unfriendly etc.

Materials, processes, sources:
Published weather data for region.
Data obtained from nearest weather station.
Solar charts, for example, cylindrical sun chart.
See Appendix A.1.a: Mazria[8]; Koenigsberger[9].
Solar radiation calculator and sliding calculator.
See Appendix A.1.a: Mazria[8].

Man-made and cultural factors

A. Site values, rights and restraints

Materials, processes, sources:
Local authorities/agencies (county and/or city): building department, engineering department, transport and roads department, health department, town-planning department.
Private or public utilities, for example, post office.
Deeds office (county assessors – USA).
Factory inspectors.
Local authority building by-laws/regulations.
Organisation providing for building funding, for example, building society.
Insurance company.
Licensing authorities.
Fire brigade.

Data required:

(a) Determine municipal valuation, market price.

(b) Obtain existing drawings if available; dimensions, shape and area of site; exact position of boundaries.

(c) Status of property: form of ownership, easements, restrictions, rights of way, rights of access, zoning, density, floor space index, building lines, height restrictions, parking requirements, consents already received.

(d) History of site: rights of public and adjoining owners; public and private intentions for future use of site; possible conflicts; boundaries and party walls and fences (ownership and condition); preservation orders on existing buildings or trees.

(e) Ascertain what consents are required and from which authorities they must be obtained; demolition requirements.

Limitations/danger signals:

— Adjacent sites that enjoy any easements against the site in question, for example, relating to drains and sewers or possibly a right to draw water from a well on the site.

— Possibility that planning permission for the project in question may not be given by the local authority or any other body from which consent must be obtained.

— Size or shape of site not suitable for type of proposed development and/or possible future expansion.

B. The surrounding area

Materials, processes, sources:
City and county land use and street maps.
City future development plans.

Data required:

(a) Existing land uses and functions; possible future changes; historic trails and passageways; historic buildings; conservation areas.

(b) Relationship to surroundings; adequacy of local facilities: transport, schools, shops, postal service, housing etc. What is within walking distance?

(c) Relationship to users, labour force, markets, existing sources of supply and services.

(d) Quality/character of neighbourhood and suitability for proposed project; effect of project on neighbourhood.

(e) Existing street layout and possible future changes; accessibility for all purposes; parking facilities.

(f) Possibility of extending site in future if necessary, for example, possibility of purchasing adjoining land.

Limitations/danger signals:

— Future motorway or highway schemes that might affect project.
— Undesirable features in vicinity: tanneries, airports, railway sidings, highways or roads carrying heavy traffic, refuse dumps, radioactivity, high tension wires etc.
— Lack of public transport.
— Lack of diversity.
— Lack of schools, police, libraries, amusement, employment.
— Socially unattractive area.

C. Adjacent properties and existing buildings

Data required:

(a) Outline, location, elevations, type, condition and use of buildings on adjacent properties.
(b) Possible fire hazards; possible restraints, for example, unwanted shadows.
(c) Plans, elevations and construction details of existing buildings.
(d) Investigate condition and structural defects: signs of dry rot, beetles, damp patches, settlement cracks, loose plaster; condition of services and possibility of extension.

Materials, processes, sources:
Visual observation; site and area survey.

Limitations/danger signals:

— Buildings and trees on adjacent properties casting unwanted shadows particularly during colder months when sun is low.
— Existing buildings in vicinity showing signs of structural cracking.
— Undesirable views.
— Adjacent vacant or underused land which is vulnerable to change.

D. Services

Data required:

(a) Position, size and depth of public sewers and stormwater drains.
(b) Utility services available, for example, gas, water, electricity and telephone; positions, sizes, pressures, type of connections and type of supply (overhead or underground).
(c) Authority responsible for utility services; special requirements; costs for service and installation.
(d) Availability of and access to special services: rubbish removal, fire protection and other emergency services, street maintenance (for example, snow removal) etc.
(e) Potential for use of natural energy sources, for example, solar, wind and water.

A.3 Photographic illustrations

The following series of photographs will help to illustrate some of the many aspects of library design. Two things must be noted, however: first, that in the space available it is possible to include only a few examples of possible solutions, and that those shown are not necessarily the best alternative in each case; secondly, that words and photographs are not architecture. The quality of the spaces, the lighting and acoustics, the furniture and the finishes, and their effectiveness for the users can only be experienced, fairly examined and evaluated within the reality of the building itself.

a. Types of library

Two contrasting libraries are illustrated. One is a small public library that is a conversion of an older building; the other is a modern university library. The Chester House Library (Figs 3.1-3.3) consisted originally of five tumble-down buildings of different date, style and construction which have been very successfully restored and converted. For a comprehensive study of this building, including a detailed description of the interesting computer-controlled book-issuing system used, see *The Architects' Journal*, 27 April 1977.

Sedgewick Undergraduate Library at the University of British Columbia (Figs 3.4-3.8) is an addition, in a very limited area, to an existing library. To solve a difficult problem the architects built the two floors of the library below both ground level and an existing pedestrian mall, and opened it onto a sunken court. The bases of existing trees have been encased in large brick drums that penetrate both floors. This is an excellent example of its type: the layout, traffic flow and lighting are all highly successful. For detailed studies of this building see *The Architectural Review*, August 1976 and Appendix A.1.b: Mason.

3.1

3.3

3.2

3.4

Fig. 3.1 *The High Street side of Chester House Library. The doorways are played down and are intended to be used only as emergency exit doors. (Architects: FWB and Mary Charles. Photographer: Martin Charles)*

Fig. 3.2 *Part of the L-shaped adult lending library. This contains the reference collection, the microfiche catalogue and microfiche reader. On the left is the informal reading area in the new entrance porch. (Architects: FWB and Mary Charles. Photographer: Martin Charles)*

Fig. 3.3 *Part of the children's library. This is reached directly from the entrance area and is divided, by a large brick chimney, into two spaces. The domestic scale of this part contrasts appropriately with the lofty spaces of the adult library. (Architects: FWB and Mary Charles. Photographer: Martin Charles)*

Fig. 3.4 *The view across terraced open-court, between the existing and new buildings, towards the main entrance of the Sedgewick Undergraduate Library. The large expanses of glass are protected by overhangs containing plant boxes. (Architects: Rhone and Iredale)*

Figs. 3.5-3.6 a, b *The simple and ingenious use of the underground concept can be seen from the plans. The solid north and south ends, which are completely below ground, are the logical locations for lifts, peripheral stairs, stores, rest rooms and service areas as well as noise-producing facilities such as typing rooms. (Architects: Rhone and Iredale)*

Fig. 3.7 *To reach the circulation desk users pass through one of six turnstile entrance and inspection points each of which can be closed off by rolling grilles (seen in the background) for flexibility of control. When all are lowered the working areas of the library are closed off from the entrance facilities – study, snack, rest and smoking areas – which remain in use after-hours. (Architects: Rhone and Iredale. Photographer: Selwyn Pullan)*

Fig. 3.8 *Carpeted platforms and 900 mm square hassocks are provided throughout the building. They create an informal reading area. Four-colour supergraphics decorate all solid walls in the library. (Architects: Rhone and Iredale. Photographer: Selwyn Pullan)*

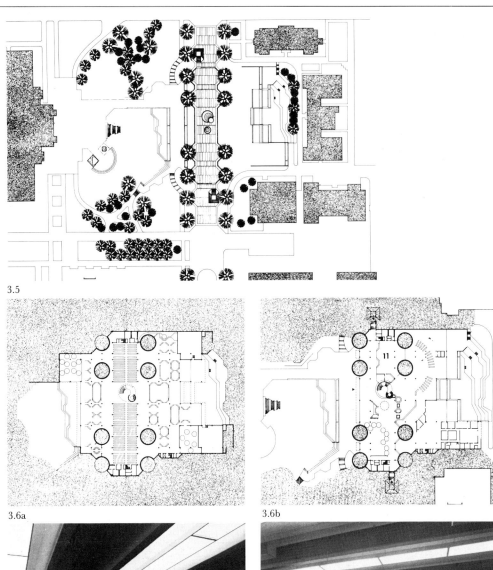

3.5

3.6a

3.6b

3.7

3.8

3.9

Fig. 3.9 *Clear signage and attractive planting at the entrance. A ramp for use by the disabled is located unobtrusively behind the plant box. (Haringey Central Library, London. Photographer: Richard Bryant)*

Fig. 3.10 *When considering requirements for parking, bicycles must not be forgotten. (Photographer: de Burgh Galwey)*

Fig. 3.11 *Enclosed courtyards used as reading areas must not permit exits from the building which by-pass the control counter. Courtyards can help to bring more natural light and ventilation to public spaces but they should not be so large that they interfere with the internal circulation and general functioning of the library. (West Norwood Library, London. Photographer: Sam Lambert)*

Fig. 3.12 *An enclosed courtyard with planting should be accessible for maintenance. The staff must not have to pass through the library with gardening equipment. (Portsmouth Polytechnic Library. Architect: ABK. Photographer: Antoine E. Raffoul)*

3.10

3.11

3.12

Fig. 3.13 *View of a circulation/control counter seen from the entrance area which has a sensible studded rubber floor. On the wall to the left is a form of building directory (note also the large signs within the library space). The existence and function of the various departments and facilities must be made clear to users: the easier the library is to use, the more it will be used. (Haringey Central Library, London. Photographer: Richard Bryant)*

Fig. 3.14 *The same circulation counter seen from within the library looking towards the entrance. On the right is the information counter and photocopying facilities.*

Fig. 3.15 *The information counter with closed-circuit television screens for keeping the whole library under surveillance as well as screens for on-line data bases.*

Fig. 3.16 *The circulation counter in a small public library that uses the card charging system. The separate information desk can be seen in the background. (John Barnes Library, Holloway, London. Library Design and Engineering. Photographer: Alexandra Studio)*

Fig. 3.17 *The circulation counter in a small public library that uses a computerised charging system. The light pen unit, used to transmit information to the computer, can be seen set into the counter on the right-hand side of the photograph. (West Sussex County Library. Library Design and Engineering. Photographer: Alexandra Studio)*

Fig. 3.18 *Issue and return counters are sometimes separated. The issue counter of the lending department of the Birmingham Central Library. (Architects: John Madin Design Group. Photographer: Sam Lambert)*

3.13

3.14

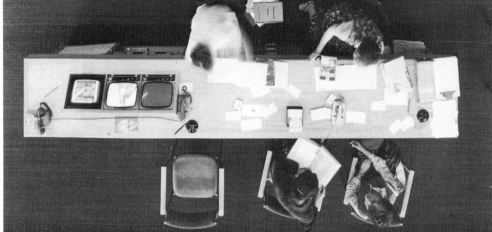

3.15

3.16

3.17

3.18

3.20

3.19

3.21

Fig. 3.19 *A large rectangular circulation desk enclosing the circulation department work area. This allows plenty of space for the many functions it serves as well as for expansion. The four-channel manned exit control can be seen in the background. (Edinburgh University Library. Architects: Sir Basil Spence, Glover and Ferguson. Photographer: Henk Snoek)*

Fig. 3.20 *A long linear control desk with a circulation department work area behind – a system used in many large libraries. (Leicester University Library. Architects: Castle Park Dean Nook. Photographer: John Donat)*

Fig. 3.21 *An exit control system using microwave electronics. Small self-adhesive sensitised tags are attached to library material (concealed in book spines, record sleeves, cassette containers etc). Scanners, housed in pedestals and linked to an alarm system (visual or audible), create an electronic field which is activated at the issue counter by tags that have not been desensitised. (Senelco Surveillance Systems)*

Fig. 3.22 *Housed in a compact and unobtrusive pedestal (approximately 1 m high and 250 mm square) scanners create an electronic field up to 6 m wide close to the library exit. (Senelco Surveillance Systems)*

3.22

Fig. 3.23 *A book being desensitised in a small machine at the issue counter. (3M Book Detection System)*

Fig. 3.24 *In this system (3M) an alarm rings and the exit push bar is automatically locked if the sensing device is activated*

Fig. 3.25 *In some libraries security is still maintained by guards at exits controlled by turnstiles. This system tends to be aesthetically unattractive and not entirely effective. (Hull University Library. Architects: Castle Park Dean Nook. Photographer: Bill Toomey)*

Fig. 3.26 *A small catalogue adjacent to the enquiries counter in a public library. (Redcar District Library. Architects: ABK. Photographer: John Donat)*

3.23   3.24

3.25

3.26

3.27

3.28

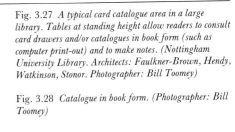

Fig. 3.27 *A typical card catalogue area in a large library. Tables at standing height allow readers to consult card drawers and/or catalogues in book form (such as computer print-out) and to make notes. (Nottingham University Library. Architects: Faulkner-Brown, Hendy, Watkinson, Stonor. Photographer: Bill Toomey)*

Fig. 3.28 *Catalogue in book form. (Photographer: Bill Toomey)*

Fig. 3.29 *A typical small one-room public library. (West Sussex County Library. Library Design and Engineering. Photographer: Alexandra Studio)*

Fig. 3.30 *The spacious lending department of the Haringey Central Libary (see also Figs. 3.13 and 3.14) which allows for future expansion. The non-fiction and reference book stocks have been integrated in this area, and the main reading/study area (with no books) is on the gallery overhead. Readers generally prefer to use the few seats provided between the shelves. (Haringey Central Library, London. Photographer: Richard Bryant)*

Fig. 3.31 *The Sutton Central Library which is divided into activity centres where specialised staff deal with the requirements of their specific subjects. Shown here is the top floor containing non-fiction on loan (divided into subject areas), reference material and a stack area. Floors are on two levels with the main activities in the central area and quiet, more private, activity on galleries (raised approximately 1 m) around the sides. On this floor the central area is dominated by electronic devices and microform equipment. (Photographer: Richard Bryant)*

3.29

3.30

3.31

3.32

3.33

3.34

3.35

3.36

3.37

Fig. 3.32 *The same area as Fig. 3.31, but viewed from the raised gallery. The backs of bookcases on the low level form fronts to study tables on the gallery. Natural light comes through the ceiling via rooflights freeing the walls for shelving.*

Fig. 3.33 *The reference department of the new Milton Keynes Central Library with electronic detection equipment at the control point. (Photographer: Richard Bryant)*

Fig. 3.34 *Periodicals area with comfortable seating is part of the lending area in this library. (Chichester College of Technology. Library Design and Engineering. Photographer: Alexandra Studio)*

Fig. 3.35 *The open volume Redcar Public Library: the adult and children's lending departments, including the periodical area seen in this photograph, are on ground level and the reference department is at first floor level. (Redcar District Library. Architects: ABK. Photographer: John Donat)*

Fig. 3.36 *The music section of the audio-visual department of Haringey Central Library. This section contains sheet music, records, cassettes, art books and prints, all of which are available for loan; also available are a number of pieces of special equipment, microform readers and a large television set. (Photographer: Richard Bryant)*

Fig. 3.37 *The control desk of the audio-visual department illustrated in Fig. 3.36. (Photographer: Richard Bryant)*

Fig. 3.38 *A circular seating arrangement in a music and arts area where plug-in headphone units are connected to one of five record and three cassette decks. Sutton Central Library – see also Figs. 3.31 and 3.32. (Photographer: Richard Bryant)*

Fig. 3.39 *The music room in West Norwood Library. Absence of doors enables music to be heard throughout the library, normally with enjoyment. Earphones are provided for private listening. (Photographer: Sam Lambert)*

Fig. 3.40 *The very large and complex reference section of the Birmingham Public Library is divided into nine subject departments spread over four floors. Shown here is the local studies department with a long service counter behind which are the closed-access bookstacks. The cast iron staircase, leading to the local studies archive above, is from the old library. (Architects: John Madin Design Group)*

Fig. 3.41 *An example of a special collection/rare book room. The Dickens Collection in the Portsmouth Central Library. (Library Design and Engineering. Photographer: Alexandra Studio)*

3.38

3.39

3.41

3.40

3.42

3.43

Fig. 3.42 *A small public library with children's and adults' libraries in one space. A separate activity room is provided for the children. (Great Missenden Library. Photographer: Giles Smith)*

Fig. 3.43 *A small separate children's room with various forms of seating. (Wellgate Library, Dundee)*

Fig. 3.44 *The children's department in the Milton Keynes Central Library. Curtains are used to screen off story-telling space. (Photographer: Richard Bryant)*

Figs. 3.45 and 3.46 *A story-pit which can be filled with large plywood blocks to form a stage with its own curtains and basic stage lighting. This multi-purpose space is used at times for creative activities (when the floor is covered with protective material). (Sutton Library. Photographer: Richard Bryant)*

3.44

3.46

3.45

Fig. 3.47 *Open-access stacks in a large university library. Note the relationship of the bookstack ranges to the column grid. (Exeter Library, Central Hall. Architect: Louis Kahn. Photographer: Cervin Robinson)*

Fig. 3.48 *Main cross aisles in an open-access stack. The shelves are of a steel cantilever system with a light wood end panel. (Bomefa. Pilkington Library, Loughborough University)*

Fig. 3.49 *Wider than normal aisle space for periodicals racks in the bookstack area of Nottingham University Library. (Architects: Faulkner-Brown, Hendy, Watkinson, Stonor. Photographer: Sam Lambert)*

Fig. 3.50 *Academic libraries are often divided into subject departments each of which has a service point manned by specialist subject librarians. It is preferable for readers to pass through bookstacks on the way to reading areas rather than vice versa. (Edinburgh University Library. Architects: Sir Basil Spence, Glover and Ferguson. Photographer: Henk Snoek)*

Fig. 3.51 *The central reading area in one of the reference departments of the Birmingham Central Library. This type of void (or well) and balcony is widely used in large libraries. They often provide much needed spatial relief and can be very successful if well handled. Problems, however, include the difficulty of controlling airborne sound and possible loss of flexibility or increase of circulation distances. (Architects: John Madin Design Group. Photographer: Sam Lambert)*

Fig. 3.52 *Comfortable seating helps to create a relaxed atmosphere in this fiction lounge. (Exeter Library. Architect: Louis Kahn. Photographer: Cervin Robinson)*

3.47

3.48

3.50

3.49

3.51

3.52

3.54

3.53

3.55

Fig. 3.53 *Formal seating at a long reading table with a central screen. When planning seating it is important to consider how it is placed and how it will be used. For example, tables seating six or more are rarely fully occupied: although the space provided may be physically adequate, such tables are generally psychologically unsatisfactory. Note ventilation trunking with air nozzles – noise and irritation of air blasting from these cause uncomfortable conditions for readers. (Portsmouth Polytechnic Library. Architects: ABK. Photographer: John Donat)*

Fig. 3.54 *Open carrels with built-in lighting and power points for audio-visual equipment. This type of screening tends to have the feeling of 'blinkers' and the pinwheel layout or U-shaped screen open on one side is generally preferred by users. (Bognor Regis College Library. Library Design and Engineering. Photographer: John Donat)*

Fig. 3.55 *Reading tables on an outside wall at the end of stack ranges. Chairs positioned with their backs to a walkway are generally perceived as unprotected and are often not fully used. (Portsmouth Polytechnic Library. Architects: ABK. Photographer: Martin Charles)*

Fig. 3.56 *Another form of seating against an outside wall. Here backs are protected and windows provide a view to the outside. (Nottingham University Library. Architects: Faulkner-Brown, Hendy, Watkinson, Stonor. Photographer: Bill Toomey)*

Fig. 3.57 *Specially designed carrel unit for microform readers. (Portsmouth Polytechnic Library. Architects: ABK. Photographer: Martin Charles)*

3.57

3.56

Fig. 3.58 *These proprietary carrel units for audio-visual usage are 1,450 × 610 mm deep, which is longer than normal. They are fitted with lockable drawers and pull-out shelves for projectors. (Worthing Central Library. Library Design and Engineering. Photographer: Alexandra Studio)*

Fig. 3.59 *Special carrels with provision for a variety of audio-visual equipment in the very interesting library of Millfield School. (Architects: Jeremy and Caroline Gould. Photographer: John Donat)*

Fig. 3.60 *An enclosed and lockable carrel. This type of facility should be close to the book collections but in areas which are quiet and relatively private. (Nottingham University Library. Architects: Faulkner-Brown, Hendy, Watkinson, Stonor. Photographer: Sam Lambert)*

3.58

3.59

3.60

3.61

3.62

3.64

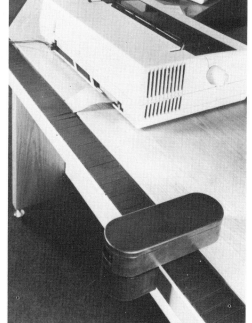

3.63

3.65

Fig. 3.61 *Technical services in one large space. Cataloguers in the foreground are separated from accessioning staff by a screen (in the background) and by the columns and bookshelf units (on the right). This area is very open and staff have no visual privacy. (Edinburgh University Library. Architects: Sir Basil Spence, Glover and Ferguson)*

Fig. 3.62 *A typical workstation arrangement calls for book trolleys on the right (or left) side with desk surface and shelves for reference material. Space may be required for a typewriter. (Hull University. Architects: Castle Park Dean Nook. Photographer: Bill Toomey)*

Fig. 3.63 *There are various proprietary modular office furniture systems on the market which allow workstations to be built up from a combination of standard elements. Some are of free-standing units while others are based on screens (or panels) from which components are hung or to which they are attached. Sound-absorbent panels can be used to enclose stations where noisy equipment is used. (Open Plan)*

Fig. 3.64 *Libraries increasingly depend on electrical and communication equipment such as microform readers, computer terminals, audio-visual machines, closed-circuit television, word-processors and copying machines. Flexible provision of outlets in almost any part of a space can be provided for by using some form of trunking – underfloor, ceiling, skirting or dado trunking – possibly together with adjustable power poles (illustrated here) which can be easily re-positioned.*

Fig. 3.65 *Many of the modular furniture systems make provision for 'wire management' by integrating cables, wiring and lighting into the components. (Hille International)*

Fig. 3.66 *A typical bindery. Most libraries send their books out for binding but some large libraries have their own facilities. As much of the work is done by hand, elaborate equipment is generally not required. (York University Library. Architects: Robert Matthew, Johnson-Marshall and Partners. Photographer: Keith Gibson)*

Fig. 3.67 *A staff room with kitchen and bar counter. (West Norwood Library. Photographer: Sam Lambert)*

Fig. 3.68 *A small lecture/viewing theatre with projection booth in the Millfield School Library and resources centre. (Architects: Jeremy and Caroline Gould. Photographer: John Donat)*

Fig. 3.69 *An exhibition area. There are various proprietary knock-down modular display systems on the market and some make provision for lighting to be incorporated. (Nottingham University Library. Architects: Faulkner-Brown, Hendy, Watkinson, Stonor. Photographer: Bill Toomey)*

Fig. 3.70 *The design of exhibition cases for rare book/manuscript displays requires very careful attention to detail. They must be constructed to allow the passage of filtered air and to contain sufficient renewable open-textured material to stabilise relative humidity. Specialist advice on these aspects, and on the difficult problem of lighting, should be obtained. (Charlotte Square, Edinburgh, Public Record Office)*

3.66

3.67

3.68

3.69

3.70

3.71

3.72

3.74

3.75

Figs. 3.71 *and* 3.72 *With the type of illumination shown in these examples (with the light source directly in front of readers) care must be taken that the lamp is not visible. Another problem is indirect glare and veiling reflections caused by light reflected up into the eyes from the reading surface: if carrels have side screens from which the light can be reflected back to the reading surface, a prismatic lens below the light source can solve the problem. The best solution is illumination from either side or, ideally, both sides. (3.71 Radcliffe Science Library, Oxford. Architects: Jack Lankester/Alastair Milne; 3.72: Trinity College, Dublin. Architects: ABK. Photographer: Deegan)*

Fig. 3.73 *Individually controlled and adjustable reading-lamps are sometimes provided. One of the problems with this type of arrangement is that a fitting adjusted to suit the reader using it may cause intolerable glare for someone else. (Trinity College, Dublin. Architects: ABK. Photographer: Norman McGrath)*

Fig. 3.74 *A grid pattern of luminaires recessed into the ceiling provides general lighting suitable for the reading area and display shelves. This system is generally very flexible as it allows bookstack ranges to run in either direction. The minimum clearance required from the top of the stack to the ceiling is usually about 900 mm. (Architects: Sir Basil Spence, Glover and Ferguson. Photographer: A. L. Hunter)*

Fig. 3.75 *Fluorescent luminaires running parallel to stack ranges. To get even lighting on both stack faces fittings must run down the centre of the aisle. This makes it virtually impossible to change centre-to-centre spacing of the stack ranges without altering all the lighting. Little clearance is required above the stacks. (Edinburgh University Library. Architects: Sir Basil Spence, Glover and Ferguson. Photographer: Henk Snoek)*

Fig. 3.76 *Fluorescent luminaires running perpendicular to stack ranges allow flexibility of centre-to-centre spacing. Centre-to-centre spacing of rows of luminaires should be between 1.4-1.8 m. Clearance required between the top of the stack and the ceiling is approximately 300 mm. Note that the majority of luminaires – placed within the ceiling coffers – are out of line of sight (see also Fig. 3.77). (Nottingham University Library. Architects: Faulkner-Brown, Hendy, Watkinson, Stonor. Photographer: Sam Lambert)*

Fig. 3.77 *General lighting combined with localised lighting: individual canopy fittings that are an integral part of the shelving units. If flexibility of stack spacing is required provision must be made for a flexible power supply by means of underfloor or ceiling trunking. (Norwich Public Library. Architect: David Percival. Photographer: Bill Toomey)*

Fig. 3.78 *Canopy lighting combined with spotlights. (Pimlico Library, London. Architects: Darbourne & Darke. Photographer: Martin Charles)*

3.76

3.77

3.78

3.79

3.80

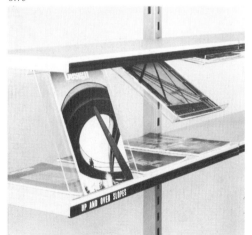

3.81

3.82

3.83

3.84

Fig. 3.79 *Basic components of a proprietary modular shelving system. (3.79-3.84: Library Design and Engineering. Photographer: Alexandra Studio)*

Fig. 3.80 *The same system as shown in Fig. 3.79 complete with timber end panel and fascia, as well as a study/reading unit.*

Figs. 3.81-3.84 *Some of the many ancillary components which can be used in conjunction with the system illustrated in Figs. 3.79 and 3.80: clear perspex up-and-over periodicals slopes with storage for back numbers behind; suspended storage for transparencies with illuminated viewing panel; pamphlet boxes suspended from cross rail; pull-out reference shelf.*

Figs. 3.85-3.87 *Alternative ways of displaying current periodicals. The up-and-over system provides storage for back numbers behind the display slope. (Fig. 3.85: Pilkington Library, Loughborough University. Bomefa. Fig. 3.86: Libraco)*

Fig. 3.88 *Newspaper display rack on a metal stand. This model accommodates eight files and is 710 mm high, 740 mm wide and 680 mm deep.*

Fig. 3.89 *A kinderbox unit for the display of large and thin books for small children. (Libraco)*

Fig. 3.90 *Two-tier and double-sided record browser. (Worthing Central Library. Library Design and Engineering. Photographer: Alexandra Studio)*

3.85

3.86

3.87

3.89

3.88

3.90

3.91

3.95

3.92

3.93

3.94

Fig. 3.91 *Atlas storage unit with sloping top. (Library Design and Engineering. Photographer: Alexandra Studio)*

Fig. 3.92 *Compact book storage: the 'floating gangway' principle where a low-geared cranking system requiring minimum pressure to operate provides mobility of units.*

Figs. 3.93-3.95 *Three alternative mechanical handling systems for library materials: small lift and small vertical conveyor both used for books and other bulky items; an electric car transporter for horizontal and vertical movement. (D.D. Lamson)*

A.4 The main consultants

Only persons appropriately qualified and registered under the Architects' Registration Acts may use the title architect. Although this may be a guarantee of a certain level of competence, it is certainly no more than that. Architects vary greatly in their outlook and approach: some are general practitioners, others are specialists; some are artists, others are businessmen. It is, therefore, very important for a client to find the right architect for the specific project in question.

One way of doing this is by approaching the Clients' Advisory Service of the RIBA (see 'Professional bodies' below) for advice. When the field has been narrowed to a few firms it is wise to visit each one to meet and talk to the partners and to see how each office is organised as well as examples of the firm's work before making a final decision.

In the USA there is a new way of matching client with designer: the public sector has recently been obliged by legislation to advertise its requirements for architectural services to which interested architects may respond. As a result the American Institute of Architects has been forced to abandon its prohibition of competitive bidding for projects by member practices. Without radical changes in Government policy this could not happen in the UK.

Responsibilities and services

The architect's primary professional responsibility is to act as the client's adviser and additionally to administer the building contract fairly between client and contractor. Architects generally provide a variety of services to meet the special requirements of their clients. The work normally undertaken during the course of a building project is described by the RIBA as 'basic services' and it may be summarised as follows (the work described is usually undertaken together with other appointed consultants):

1 Preliminary services which include: discussing, reviewing and evaluating the client's brief; providing advice on how to proceed and on the need for other consultants' services; site visit and initial appraisal; and preparation of outline timetable.

2 Analysis of requirements and preparation of feasibility studies.

3 Outline proposals and an estimate of construction cost for the client's preliminary approval.

4 Development of a scheme design together with cost estimate; attending to applications for planning permission.

5 Detail design and co-ordination of design work done by other consultants and specialists; attending to applications for building approvals.

6 Advising on and arranging for tenders and contract.

7 Contract administration and site supervision up to completion of the works.

Details of these and other services which architects may be called upon to provide, either to augment the basic services or as a separate service, for example, the preparation of the brief (which in many cases is considered an additional service) may be obtained from the RIBA.

Fees

Until recently architects' fees were based on a set of standard mandatory figures prepared by the RIBA. Various fee options are now available and which is used depends on factors including the service to be provided, the size and type of project and negotiations between client and architect. The three basic options used are:

1 Percentage of total construction cost. The RIBA has separate recommended fee scales for new works and works to existing buildings. These consist of sliding scales for different classes of work – the higher the cost of the project and the less complex the building type, the lower the percentage.

2 Time charges based on hourly rates for principals and other technical staff.

3 In certain cases architect and client may agree on a lump sum.

Professional bodies

The Royal Institute of British Architects (RIBA)
66 Portland Place
London W1N 4AD
Tel. 01-580 5533

The Royal Incorporation of Architects in Scotland (RIAS)
15 Rutland Square
Edinburgh EH1 2BE
Tel. 031-229 7205

The Royal Society of Ulster Architects
2 Mount Charles
Belfast BT7 1NZ

The American Institute of Architects
1735 New York Avenue, NW
Washington DC 20006

Most architectural firms in the UK are members of the RIBA and are governed by its code of professional conduct. The services which can be provided by architects, the conditions of appointment and the scale of fees charged by them for particular services are described in *Architect's Appointment* and in the *Directory of Practices* which also includes the names and addresses of member practices and the types of work they undertake. These and other publications produced by the RIBA are available from their bookshop at the London address. The Institute provides a client's advisory service. Their library contains a comprehensive collection of publications on architecture and is open to the general public for reference.

b. Building surveyors

Services

A chartered building surveyor is qualified by examination and experience as a member of the Royal Institution of Chartered Surveyors, and can provide an advisory or consultancy service on various aspects of the construction and economics of buildings. This includes:

1 the diagnosis of building defects and advice on remedial work;

2 the planning and implementation of maintenance work;

3 project management; and

4 structural surveys of all types of property.

Fees

Fees are often based on the time involved but in some cases, such as the supervision of building work, they may be based on a percentage of the overall cost of the project. The Royal Institution of Chartered Surveyors publishes *Conditions of Engagement for Building Surveying Services* which sets out in detail the type of work carried out. Potential clients should consult this publication, and a fee for the service to be provided should be agreed prior to instructions being given.

Professional body

The Royal Institution of Chartered Surveyors (RICS)
12 Great George Street
Parliament Square
London SW1P 3AD
Tel. 01-222 7000
and:
7 Manor Place
Edinburgh EH3 7DN
Tel. 031-225 7078

c. Engineers

Services

There are two main groups of engineers: civil and structural, and services engineers. The first group form part of the design team to assist with the design and calculations for elements such as foundations, retaining walls, columns, beams, slabs and roofs whether these are of reinforced concrete, steel or timber. On some projects (for example, those consisting largely of structural elements) the engineer may be employed as the principal designer.

Services engineers are appointed as members of the design team to assist with the design of environmental control aspects such as lighting, heating and air-conditioning, and mechanical services. As these items can represent a high proportion of building costs, the appointment of the required consultants at an early enough stage for them to participate in the briefing process and feasibility studies is to be recommended.

Fees

For details of fees in relation to services provided contact the Association of Consulting Engineers or the appropriate institution.

Professional bodies

The Association of Consulting Engineers
1st Floor
Alliance House
12 Caxton Street
London SW1H 0QL
Tel. 01-222 6557
This is a professional association of independent consulting engineers. It provides an advisory service and, if requested to do so, will nominate suitable members for particular purposes. Publications are produced describing the services provided by consulting engineers, the conditions of engagement and the scale of fees.

The Chartered Institution of Building Services
Delta House
222 Balham High Road
London SW12 9BS
Tel. 01-675 5211
The Institution promotes the science and practice of heating, ventilation, air-conditioning, domestic hot water engineering and all other building services. Enquiry and advisory services are available.

The American Institute of Consulting Engineers
345 E 47th Street
New York
NY 10017

d.   Interior designers

Services

These professionals generally provide the same design and technical services that an architect provides but restrict their work to interiors only.

An interior designer may work on a project in association with other professionals (as part of a design team), or may in certain cases (non-structural refurbishment) be the sole consultant. In all cases the interior designer may be appointed by agreement for one or more of the following progressive stages:

1 A study of the client's requirements and the scope of work; ascertaining feasibility and advising on the need for other specialist consultants. The preparation of preliminary proposals including initial assessment of cost and programme.

2 The preparation of detailed proposals and the necessary working drawings and specifications required for determining the contract cost. The invitation of tenders from approved contractors.

3 The submission of a report on tenders; and advising on the selection of contractors etc; supervision of the contract.

An interior design consultant may also be commissioned in an advisory capacity or for part of the whole normal service including the preparation of feasibility studies and reports, detail surveys etc.

Fees

There are three primary ways in which consultancy services are charged:

1 a percentage basis where an agreed percentage figure (usually on a sliding scale and between 15-10 or less per cent) is applied to the whole cost of the works plus remuneration for expenses;

2 a time basis where agreed time rates are levied plus expenses (small jobs are usually done on this basis); or

3 a lump sum basis where a total fee is agreed for the services specified.

Professional bodies

The British Institute of Interior Design
Lenton Lodge
Wollaton Hall Drive
Nottingham NG8 1AF
Tel. 0602-701205

This is a professional organisation of interior designers, designers in related disciplines, crafts persons/designers and persons who provide a service in one or more specific areas within the interior environment. The Institute can supply details of services, fee scales etc, and will supply clients with a short list of interior designers of appropriate experience for specific projects.

The American Institute of Interior Designers
730 5th Avenue
New York
NY 10019

e. Landscape consultants

The term landscape consultant refers to the following three groups of professionals:
1   Landscape architects who are trained in the planning and design of all types of outdoor spaces. They use knowledge of the natural elements of the landscape, its materials and components, to create the spatial and aesthetic elements of the new environment. Many practitioners are also qualified in other disciplines such as horticulture, planning or architecture. They may develop projects into contracts and supervise their execution on site.
2   Landscape scientists who are concerned with the physical and biological principles and processes which underlie the planning, design and management of natural resources. They have the ability to relate their scientific knowledge to the practical problems of landscape work which can range from small-scale site surveys to ecological assessments. Landscape scientists usually have a science background such as ecology, often with specialist skills such as soil science, hydrology or botany.
3   Landscape managers are specialists employing management techniques in the long-term care and development of new and existing landscapes. They usually have a degree in horticulture, forestry or agriculture together with further training in land management or other related disciplines.

Services

The landscape consultant's work involves both the existing landscape and the design and implementation of new landscapes and is generally associated with other professionals such as architects, planners, ecologists and engineers. The scale of work undertaken can vary considerably from designing a small courtyard or settings for all kinds of buildings to designing recreation facilities and preparing landscape plans for large areas.

The services provided may take the form of purely advisory work or may include surveys, appraisal, implementation and management. When engaged on a typical commission related to building work the landscape consultant may perform some, or all, of the following services:
1   the appraisal of site conditions;
2   the survey of the site to provide accurate information about the nature of the land and soil, including the existing features, the condition and lifespan of trees and shrubs, and the types of plants already growing or likely to grow;
3   the preparation of preliminary sketch plans and approximate estimates for the client's approval;
4   the preparation of all drawings and specifications required for the execution of the work;

5 the preparation of contract documents (other than bills of quantities); also obtaining and advising on tenders;

6 the administration of the contract and supervision of the work on site;

7 checking and certifying accounts (but not measurement and valuation of the work); and

8 the submission of plans for necessary approvals by public bodies.

Fees

There are two main methods of determining remuneration: on the time basis or on the percentage basis, with reimbursement for expenses being added to the fee in both cases. Full details may be obtained from the Landscape Institute.

The percentage basis is only applied to a contract costing £10,000 and over and is calculated from two components: a percentage figure is read off a graph against the cost of the project (that is, the higher the project cost the lower the percentage). This figure is the 'norm' which is adjusted by a coefficient based on either the form of contract or the type of job (and therefore its complexity). Some services (for example, site surveys) are specifically excluded from those within the percentage 'norm' and are charged for additionally on a time basis or negotiated sum.

Professional bodies

The Landscape Institute
12 Carlton House Terrace
London SW1Y 5AH
Tel. 01-839 4044

The Institute can provide information on conditions of engagement and professional charges and will nominate practices for commissions at the request of clients. It operates a reference library and publishes a quarterly journal, *Landscape Design*, which is available to non-members on subscription.

The American Institute of Landscape Architects
501 E San Juan Avenue
Phoenix A285012

f. Land surveyors

Services

In a world of rapidly changing technology, the services offered by land surveyors are constantly adapting and expanding to meet the needs of a wide variety of clients. The major advisory and/or consultancy services offered to those involved in new construction work include:

1 property boundary surveys;

2 area or site surveying;

3 architectural surveys, to record new and existing buildings in plan, by section or in elevation;

4 setting out of building and construction work; and

5   aerial photography and photogrammetry – orthophotomaps or the recording of historic buildings and monuments etc.

Fees

There is no fee scale for land surveying services and information on ranges of fees for specific services may be obtained from the Royal Institution of Chartered Surveyors or directly from member firms.

Professional body

The Royal Institution of Chartered Surveyors (RICS)
12 Great George Street
Parliament Square
London SW1P 3AD
Tel. 01-222 7000
and:
7 Manor Place
Edinburgh EH3 7DN
Tel. 031-225 7078
The Institution has an information centre which runs a nomination service for clients and will always give guidance on services offered or transfer a client to the appropriate divisional secretary. Various publications are available including the *Directory of Land and Hydrographic Survey Services in the United Kingdom.*

g. Quantity surveyors

Services

The quantity surveyor is the expert professional trained to assist clients and architects with construction costs, construction management and construction communications. This consultant is an important member of the briefing and design team and should be appointed at an early stage to provide some, or all, of the following services:

1   preliminary cost advice including recommendations on most economical layout, materials and methods of construction; also estimates of future maintenance and running costs;

2   estimates of the costs of alternative proposals;

3   cost planning – a specialist technique used to help all the members of the design team to arrive jointly at practical designs for a specific project and stay within the agreed budget. Also assessment of the cost implications of changes;

4   advising on contractual methods;

5   preparing bills of quantities which are used for competitive tendering and as an important element in effective cost control during construction;

6   negotiating tenders for projects planned from the outset with a single contractor. It is advisable to consider appointing an independent quantity

surveyor for advice on the financial and contractual aspects when embarking on a package deal;

7 financial management and valuing of work during construction; and

8 preparing final accounts, statements of expenditure for tax or accountancy purposes etc.

Fees

Recommended scales of fees related to the cost and complexity of the project are published by RICS. Chartered quantity surveyors will always provide estimates of their fees and RICS will give advice when necessary.

Professional body

The Royal Institution of Chartered Surveyors (RICS)
12 Great George Street
Parliament Square
London SW1P 3AD
Tel. 01-222 7000
and:
7 Manor Place
Edinburgh EH3 7DN
Tel. 031-225 7078

The Institution has an information centre which runs a nomination service for clients and will always give guidance on services offered or transfer a client to the appropriate divisional secretary. Various publications are available including leaflets describing the main services offered, and package contracts.

A.5 Briefing and design methods

There are a number of briefing and design methods which can be used to help produce different kinds of information (see Fig. A.1). Each of these techniques or tools is a separate activity for collecting, exploring, communicating, analysing, organising or evaluating information and ideas, and it is a question of not only determining whether one or more of them will be appropriate to a specific project, but also matching them with information needs. The methods used for a particular design situation will depend, amongst other things, on the people involved, on the stage one is at, on what is already known and on what one is trying to find out.

A few of the most basic, and perhaps more useful, methods are described here in broad outline. For more detailed information refer to Appendix A.1.a:

a. Literature search

To locate and retrieve published information which will not only help to lay the foundation for further investigation and for preliminary conclusions, but will also provide some of the required design data.

1 Identify the purposes for which the information is required and ascertain priorities.
2 Determine the degree of detail required – bare essentials may be sufficient initially.
3 Identify likely sources of reliable, up-to-date and relevant information. In many cases (for example, where those involved have previous experience of the relevant building type) the process may simply involve updating knowledge from literature already available in one's own library.

Literature search can be time-consuming. It is advisable to determine a timetable taking into account, not only by when the information will be required, but also a deadline beyond which the search will be discontinued. The penalty of insufficient information at a given time must be balanced against the cost of obtaining it.

Fig. A.1 *Chart indicating some of the many methods that can be employed during the briefing and design process as well as the kinds of actions for which they may be used (● = primary use, ○ = secondary use). The methods in heavy type are described in outline in this Appendix.*

◪ Indicates method which is generally a group activity

◩↓ Indicates method which generally involves users

Methods	Kinds of action / categories of information			
	Exploring design situations and/or data gathering	Searching for or generating ideas	Exploring problem structure (analysis & organisation)	Evaluation
◩ Stating objectives	●			
Literature search	●	○		
◩ Interview	●	○		
◩ Questionnaire	●	○		
◩ Observation	●	○		
Visit/study existing buildings	●	○		
◩ Data logs	●		○	
Standardised data forms	●		●	
◪ Brainstorming		●	○	
◪ Synectics		●	○	
◪ Role playing		●	○	
◪ Gaming		●	○	
Interaction matrix			●	
Correlation diagrams			●	
Functional innovation			●	
◩ Pattern language	○	●	●	○
Classification			●	
Checklists	●		○	●
Selecting criteria				●
Ranking and weighting				●
Cost planning			●	
Life cycle cost analysis			●	●
Value analysis			●	●
Cost benefit analysis			●	●
Energy accounting			●	○
◩ Post occupancy appraisal				●

The choice of sources and the applicability of data being collected must be continuously evaluated. Literature search should be stopped as soon as sufficient useful data to answer the stated questions has been gathered. Accurate references should be kept of all publications that are found to be useful for easy retrieval at a later date, and collected data should be stored in a flexible way so that new information can be readily added.

b.   Interviews

This is the most common and direct method of obtaining specific and detailed information from clients and users. Interviews serve the same purpose as questionnaires but have the advantage of direct and immediate interaction between interviewer and client or user.

Interviews may be unstructured or structured. The former – in which no

Fig. A.2 *Sources of information.*

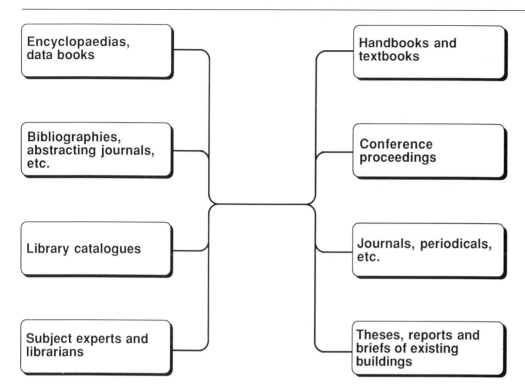

predetermined format is used – tends to be exploratory in nature and is often employed with the aim of gaining a general understanding of a problem or situation; and also of identifying the right questions to include in a questionnaire or structured interview. Structured interviews, on the other hand, follow a pre-arranged format in order to generate quick responses to specific questions.

1   Identify the kinds of information needed.
2   Identify the different types of people involved in the user situations that require exploration: client, managers, operators, consumers etc. Each type will usually have different impressions, needs, attitudes, values, preferences and problems, some of which will almost certainly be in conflict with those of the other types or groups.
3   Establish contact with and obtain the co-operation of the various groups involved.
4   Prepare a set of questions or a checklist: it is only common sense to obtain expert advice.
5   Decide who will be interviewed and make the necessary arrangements. Allow sufficient time for the predetermined questions to be answered and/or for free discussion.
6   Those interviewed should be allowed to talk spontaneously about any aspects of the activities in which they are involved that seem important to them, and encouraged to expand on those which are particularly relevant to the design situation being explored. This should be possible even in a structured interview.

7 Responses, comments and suggestions must be accurately recorded together with relevant circumstantial information: the ages, sex and expertise of those interviewed etc.

8 It is generally useful for the interviewer to have some experience of the actual user-situation being explored, and the interviews may be preceded, or followed up, by one of the observation techniques.

9 Interviewers should try to remain neutral and remember that the views and interests of the *interviewee* are being sought. (Interviewers may well have to listen to views with which they totally disagree and must not get carried away by their own points of view.)

c. Questionnaire

This serves basically the same purpose as an interview – of which it may form part – but takes the form of a written set of questions which generally require a written response. It is used to obtain a variety of usable information from large numbers of people.

1 Identify the kinds of information needed to meet specific objectives.

2 Identify the different types/groups of people involved and consider which would be most helpful in obtaining the information required.

3 Consider the types of questions which will be most suitable to get the information required: factual, informative, opinion/attitude and/or self-perception. Also consider how the answers are to be analysed.

4 Consider the form in which answers are to be given: questions can be unstructured – open-ended, encouraging descriptions of likes, dislikes, attitudes, values, behaviour and settings – or can require a fixed response: choice between two possibilities (yes/no; good/bad etc), multiple choice or ranking of set of alternatives. Although the fixed response method is obviously easier to analyse and to feed into a computer, both types of questions are often used in a single questionnaire.

When formulating questions, keep in mind that they should be short and use language that makes the meaning clear to all respondents. They should be free from any possible bias (assumptions and prejudices of the questioner), and should elicit definite, short, simple and useful answers.

Consider the design of the questionnaire: it should be laid out so that it is easy to understand and use, and does not take too long to complete. The following sequence, with questions designed to flow naturally from one to the next, is widely used:

1 Short introduction: explanation of purpose and instructions.

2 Easy-to-answer preliminary questions.

3 The main questions or body of the questionnaire.

4 Questions eliciting personal data.

Establish how the questionnaire is to be circulated, for example, in interviews, by post or at a meeting. If sent by post an accompanying explanatory letter should be enclosed.

It is essential, if the exercise is to have any validity, to draw up and circulate a pilot questionnaire to test the questions and answers, and the method of analysis, before drafting the final document.

d. Observation

It is often helpful – and sometimes essential – for designers to expose themselves to the complexities of the real situation they are designing for. The various observation techniques can be employed to get useful information about people's behaviour in a specific environment/setting: patterns of behaviour and use, space requirements and relationships, the use of furniture and equipment, dysfunction etc. Other methods (for example, interviews) will be needed to get information on the users' opinions and attitudes.

1 Identify the kinds of information needed, for example, details of the activities that take place – the different kinds as well as their frequency, duration and sequence; physical and other characteristics of the space or setting; details of the various interactions among users and between them and the setting; general data on the users involved.

2 Consider whether the study will be exploratory – to gain a general understanding; or structured – to collect specific detailed information.

3 Identify the various types of users and settings involved and consider which are to be observed: in the case of data collection for an airport design, for example, one will need to know something about the behaviour/use patterns of not only travellers but also visitors, flight crews, ground staff, administrators etc.

4 Determine what method(s) will be used:

— Direct unobtrusive observation. This may be best if users are likely to modify their actions when knowing they are being watched.

— Direct observation with the co-operation of users. It is sometimes useful to observe not only experienced users but also volunteers inexperienced in the use of the space or setting, noting their reactions and difficulties while attempting to achieve a predetermined objective.

— Participation by the observer: several sessions may be required to experience different user situations/perspectives.

— Other: tracking, behaviour-mapping etc. See Appendix A.1.a: Jones[1], Palmer[2], Sanoff[4] and Cross & Roy.

5 Obtain the necessary permission and/or co-operation needed to carry out the proposed study.

6 Decide how data – actions, difficulties, problems, impressions, ideas etc – will be recorded. Consider the possibility of using mechanical methods such as tape recording, still or time-lapse photography, videotaping or cine-filming.

Note: It must be pointed out that interviews, questionnaires and observations are research-based methods on which there is a great deal written and still some controversy. Even those trained in these methods can make mistakes and can draw the wrong conclusions from the data collected. One must, therefore, not only get expert help/advice, but also remember that while the results from these methods may give good indications of attitudes, they should be treated circumspectly and certainly not as 'the answer'.

e. Visit/study existing buildings

Before embarking on a project, a great deal can be learnt by architect, client and selected users through visits to similar organisations and buildings. There is no better way to keep abreast of new developments and obtain an insight into the problems of a particular building type, while also becoming aware of, experiencing and evaluating the many alternative solutions. While a careful study of the literature of the subject is a good introduction it is not, generally speaking, by itself sufficient.

1 Go through published information on the building type in question (in architectural journals and other professional publications).

2 Draw up a list of possible buildings to visit. When making a final selection, remember:

— It is useful to visit a few buildings that will be reasonably comparable in size and character to the one being planned and, ideally, those that offer a wide range of alternative approaches in terms of layout, construction, finishes and equipment.

— Buildings which appear to be most attractive in photographs and which are widely publicised are not necessarily the ones that function best for occupants and users. Although much can be learned from both good and bad examples, the greater the number of successful solutions one can visit the better.

— Do not attempt to visit too many buildings. It is generally advisable to keep the number down to between six and eight that can be examined carefully enough to make the exercise worthwhile.

3 Decide who will go on the visits: client, architect, selected staff and/or users. A small group made up of people with different backgrounds will provide a variety of points of view. If a specialist building consultant has been appointed his presence will be helpful as he will be able to point out satisfactory solutions of problems as well as failures. This consultant would almost certainly be able to suggest some buildings worth visiting.

4 Prepare a programme for the proposed visits allowing enough time (between a half and a full day) to study each building, see visual demonstrations and ask questions. Contact the organisations in question to arrange for the visits and for appointments with the people who should be seen.

5 Draw up a checklist of things to be looked at, points to be discussed and questions to which answers are needed:

— How was the project organised: Who prepared the brief? What sort of consultants were used? Who made various design decisions and why were they made? What would be changed with hindsight?

— Who uses the building and what kinds of functions does it house? What were the user requirements and client objectives? How well are these met by the building in question?

— How were decisions made about the interior design? What space standards were used? Is it easy to find one's way about? Are layouts of spaces satisfactory or unacceptable? Do some areas seem unduly congested and are there others where space is obviously wasted?

— What system is used – structural grid, depth of spaces etc – and how well does this suit the functions? What is the relationship of service ducts and vertical circulation to the structure? What are the ceiling heights? Are they satisfactory for the various activities involved? How practical are the materials used for floors, walls and ceilings in terms of function, quality, appearance, maintenance, sound and cost?

— What form of lighting is used and is the quality of light satisfactory for the tasks to be performed? What system is used to provide power/communication outlets? How flexible is it? What were the acoustic criteria? Is there any sound disturbance?

— What kinds of furniture and equipment are used? How were they selected? How well do they meet the criteria of function, flexibility, quality, appearance, maintenance and cost?

— To what extent has flexibility/adaptability and possible future extension been provided for? How has it been done?

— What methods will be used to collect the data required: by interviewing those involved in the briefing, by talking to staff, from observation etc?

6 Take notes during each visit. These will be helpful during subsequent discussions and for the preparation of a written report which is a useful way of organising information and ideas, and of making them available to others. It may be worthwhile taking photographs during visits to illustrate, and remind one of, specific points.

7 If it is not possible to visit some important buildings they should at least be carefully examined, ideally by studying the original brief and, if at all possible, any published post-occupancy appraisal (or evaluation as it is called in the USA). Where such material is available it is well worth studying even if the building has been visited because it provides useful supplementary information.

Post-occupancy appraisal, especially from clients' and users' points of view, has great value both as a first step in the development of a building brief – it offers the potential for obtaining the type of feedback needed to avoid past mistakes and improve the design process – and as a final step in assessing user satisfaction when it may be used for fine-tuning of the building. Although there is a growing awareness of the need for this type of study, there is at present relatively little published material available. Appraisals published in the architectural press, which range from very general descriptions to detailed case studies, do not generally attempt to examine how users relate to the building and the reasons why the building may be satisfactory or have failed in use.

f. Standardised data forms

These are used to collect, record and organise various types of routine or repetitive data (room requirements, descriptions of existing facilities, user activities, energy consumption etc). They are an ideal way of presenting detailed design information consistently for each space, system or activity in a building brief.

1 Identify the type of data that is to be collected and recorded, for example, requirements for each of the spaces in the building.

2 Determine the various categories of information that are needed, for example, activities/functions to be performed in the area, number of occupants/users, furniture and equipment, floor area, relationship to other spaces, environmental conditions, special finishes.

3 Decide on the most suitable method of recording the different types of data and prepare a layout for the form accordingly, for example, form may allow blocks within which the necessary data is filled in or may be organised as a checklist. Where possible the form should be kept to a single sheet (see Fig. A.3).

4 When a satisfactory form has been developed and drawn up have sufficient copies printed/duplicated. It may be advisable/necessary for the designers to produce a draft form after completing other studies (questionnaires, interviews, observations etc) and discussing it with the client and users before it is finalised.

5 Determine how these forms are to be completed and by whom. Forms may, for example, be attached to a questionnaire to be completed by users and the client, and finally evaluated by the designers.

g. Brainstorming

This is an extremely fast and versatile group technique which may be used at all stages of the briefing and design process to generate a large variety of ideas and/or information (sources of information, questions for interviews etc).

1 State problem clearly and simply.

Space Requirements for: (Project name/job number etc)		Department: Space name/number:		
Function of space and activities Main: Secondary:		Number of occupants/users Max: Average: Types:		No of similar rooms required:
Access and relationship to other spaces Main: Secondary:			Floor area:	Ceiling height:

Furniture and equipment		Finishes	Services	Environmental	Other
Desk		Floor:	Plumbing:	Heating, ventilation and air-conditioning:	Doors:
Counter					
Table			Electrical:		
Chairs					Windows:
Bulletin board		Walls:			
Bookshelves				Lighting:	
Storage cupboards			Fire:		Colours:
Typewriter		Ceiling:			
VDU			Communications:	Acoustics:	Storage:
Duplicating equipment					
Switchboard					

Fig. A.3 *Example of standardised form for collecting room requirements of a new building. In this case a section of the form has been organised as a checklist. In certain circumstances the whole form may best be compiled in this way.*

2 Select a group of people – small groups of between four and twelve people generally work best – to participate. Group members should ideally have some relevant knowledge/experience. No previous experience of brainstorming is necessary.

3 Select a chairman/group leader who will be able to control the session, keep the pace going and encourage a relaxed, creative atmosphere. Someone may be required to record verbal responses.

4 Decide on a time-limit for the session which should not continue for too long – between 30 and 60 minutes seems to produce the best results.

5 The following should be made clear to the participants:

— There must be no criticism or analysis of ideas.

— As many ideas as possible must be generated within the predetermined time period: the more ideas there are the more chance there is of finding some that are really useful.

— They must not worry about ideas being practical or not: responses must be spontaneous and uninhibited.

— They should feel free to combine or build on the other ideas put forward.

6 Decide on method of recording spoken ideas, for example, on a blackboard or large roll of paper. An alternative method is to allow a preliminary period for participants to write their initial ideas down, and each then reads an idea in turn. Further ideas are written on separate cards as the session proceeds.

7 Sort ideas into groups and evaluate them. The ideas themselves may not be the most valuable output: the different groups (or categories) may be used to expose a range of possible solution areas from which a serious search for a final answer can start.

h. Interaction matrix

A frequently used and most useful method for determining and/or visualising the patterns of interactions or relationships between a number of elements in a problem, for example, the connections/adjacencies required between the spaces/rooms in a building.

A matrix, in its most basic form, is a simple two-way grid on which all possible combinations, by pairs, of the elements are recorded and ranked. The matrix itself does not determine the interactions – it is rather a framework within which the information is set out and which assists the search for relationships (space, activity, organisational, functional etc) within a set of several elements.

1 Define the terms element and interaction/relationship as they apply to the specific problem, for example, room/space and adjacency/proximity.

2 Decide what, if any, form of ranking (scale of preference/priority) is to be applied, for example, in the case of adjacency of rooms the following scale may be used: 0 = not necessary, 1 = desirable or some, 2 = essential.

3 Draw up a matrix which sets out the complete range of possible interactions between every pair of elements and check for each pair whether or not interaction occurs (see Fig. A.4).

4 It is often not necessary to use both halves of a matrix, for example, when determining required adjacency between rooms – unless the direction of door swings is to be determined – and a so-called half-matrix may be used (see Fig. A.5).

5 Try to keep the number of elements to a maximum of 20 or 25 – in a very large project it is usually possible to group the elements in sub-sets. It can be difficult to complete all the judgements involved when a matrix contains large numbers of elements, and the possibility of errors is greatly increased.

A.

	A	B	C	D	E
A			●	●	
B					
C	●			●	
D	●		●		●
E				●	
	2	0	2	3	1

B.

	President	Purchasing	General sales and administration	Accounting	Production planning	Data processing	Mail and supply room	Reception
President		U	I	U	U	X	U	E
Purchasing			U	O	U	U	U	E
General sales and administration	1			I	O	E	I	I
Accounting		4	4		U	E	O	U
Production planning			4			I	U	U
Data processing	2		4	4	4		U	U
Mail and supply room			5	5				U
Reception	3	3	3					

Fig. A.4 *In matrix (A) relationships between pairs of activities are simply marked in the grid: no ranking is used. The totals at the foot of the vertical columns give the number of relationships, and thus the importance of each element. In example (B) a closeness ranking is indicated in one half of the grid (E = especially important, I = important, O = average satisfies, U = unimportant and X = undesirable) and the reason governing this is indicated in the other half (1 = use of typing pool, 2 = noise, 3 = number of visitors, 4 = movement of paper, 5 = use of supplies).*

Fig. A.5 *Matrix illustrating journeys between rooms by people working in a typical existing operating theatre suite. This can be used to decide what modifications are needed to reduce movement to a minimum and to combine the units in the most satisfactory way from all known points of view. (From* The Architects' Journal, *17 June 1964, p.1375).*

Total Journeys

Total	No.	Room
117	1	Sisters' changing room
171	2	Nurses' changing room
717	3	Surgeons' rest room
399	4	Surgeons' changing room
46	5	Superintendent's room
24	6	Medical store
395	7	Small theatre
376	8	Anaesthetic room no 1
711	9	Theatre room no 1
528	10	Sink room
488	11	Sterilising room
677	12	Scrub up room
1115	13	Ante-space and nurses' station
711	14	Theatre room no 2
376	15	Anaesthetic room no 2
395	16	Emergency theatre
254	17	Workroom and clean supply
146	18	Sterile supply room
249	19	Male staff changing room
546	20	Nurses' station
305	21	The entrance

i. Correlation diagrams

There are a variety of techniques (interaction nets, bubble and block diagrams, flow diagrams etc) which are used for displaying spatial or other relationships between elements within a design problem. Such diagrams are widely used as an intermediate step for generating the actual plan layout of a building, and for visualising all the factors and variables that have a bearing on the design process.

1 Collect and analyse data. It is generally advisable to use an interaction matrix to determine relationships/interactions.

2 In the case of the interaction net technique a preliminary diagram is drawn with elements (for example, functions or spaces) represented by symbols and arranged in a circle. Relationships/interactions are indicated by linking elements with lines which may be varied in weight (thickness) to show the relative importance of the connections. The diagram is then adjusted with elements rearranged to minimise the crossing of lines (considering the essential links first and, once these have been sorted out, the secondary ones) and to clarify the pattern of interaction, looking for strong sub-groupings or clusters of elements (see Fig. A.6).

3 Bubble diagrams are usually sketched freehand with bubbles (representing

elements drawn within each other, overlapping or separated by a link (line) depending on the relationships and connections. Lines may be used to indicate the distance between elements, the pattern of movement between elements, and/or the importance of the connection between each of them (see Fig. A.7).

4 Block diagrams, which are similar to bubble diagrams, consist of squares or rectangles – representing each space – that are drawn to scale (proportionally sized to the amount of floor area required). Each of the blocks can be cut out of paper or cardboard and shuffled around to test various arrangements.

5 A form of flow chart can be used to visualise or externalise all the factors and variables having a bearing on a particular design project. A roll of newsprint or brown paper attached to a wall can be used for this purpose. One approach is to:

   a draw up a classification of the main sub-components (elements) which are to be investigated (activites, materials etc);

   b list all the points that can be thought of, putting each under the classification that seems to make most sense;

   c establish relationships. By studying the chart, connections may be found where none seemed to exist before. For example, in preparing a chart for a children's playground the list under activities may include climbing, running, sliding, jumping; under the heading of materials one may have listed heavy canvas, which, when stretched and supported is buoyant and comparatively resilient. Thus, a link may be established between this and 'jumping', suggesting a trampoline-like structure;

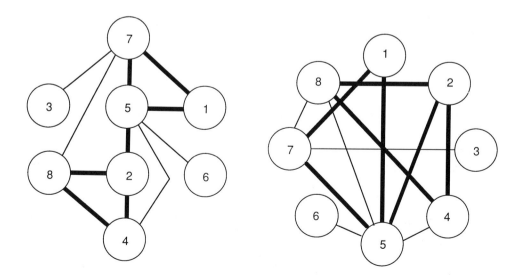

Fig. A.6 *The two basic stages of an interaction net illustrated very simply.*

Fig. A.7 *Bubble diagram used as a first step for generating actual plan layout of a building.*

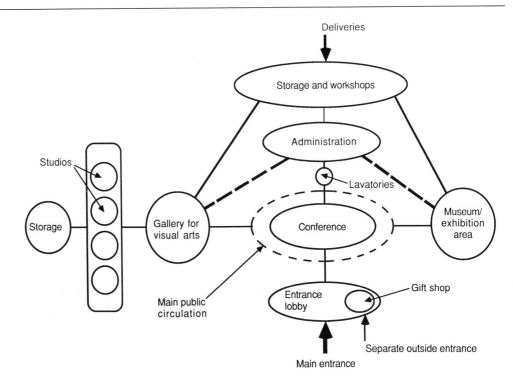

d draw lines to connect relationships and possible things to do as a result of the connections (for example, design a trampoline-like structure), as they are established. New concepts, categories, relationships and solutions/things to do are filled-in as they come to mind during the briefing/design process; then

e once this part of the chart has been more or less fully developed (it will never be complete) a second half consisting of implementation (who does what, when and how) can be added. The chart remains on the wall being altered and amended until the work has been completed.

j.   Pattern language

This is a method developed by Christopher Alexander and his associates at the Centre for Environmental Structure at Berkeley, California, which is, theoretically, supposed to allow everyone to design for themselves the places they live and work in, while simultaneously giving order to the whole environment. The language consists of a 'dictionary' containing a set of patterns each of which suggests how a specific problem, which happens over and over again in an environment or a building, can be solved (see Fig. A.8). By selecting relevant patterns from Alexander's dictionary, generating others to suit local culture and conditions, and then combining them according to the specific needs of the project in question, a design can be created.

Although it may be naive to believe that the complex buildings and environments of today's industrialised society can be designed by users working with pattern books and without the aid of professional designers, there is a great deal of value in Alexander's work. For the purposes of education, the generation of ideas, the development of awareness, and involvement during the briefing and design process, Alexander's book of patterns can be an invaluable tool not only for designers but also for clients and users.

k. Cost planning

The object of cost planning (see Fig. A.9) (usually the responsibility of the appointed quantity surveyor) is to ensure that the final cost of a building project does not exceed the client's original budget figure.

A start should be made on analysing and controlling costs as early as possible in the briefing and design process. This will avoid the costly and time-consuming changes that result when it is discovered that costs exceed the budget *after* a design has been prepared.

1 Establish cost limitations at the start of the project: the client often stipulates a limit in his initial statement (preliminary brief).

2 Prepare a realistic preliminary estimate as early as possible (usually during the feasibility phase) either to confirm that the cost limitation is realistic in terms of the stated requirements, or to enable those involved to begin the inevitable trade-offs.

3 The preliminary estimate must often be based on the requirements defined during the development of the brief:

— Space: the floor area required.

— The use to which the space will be put.

— Quality: the standard of finishes, fittings and equipment required.

— External works.

— The maintenance and running costs the client is prepared to meet.

The estimate is generally calculated by using a cost per m^2 of floor area, based on an analysis of costs of the same, or similar, requirements in actual construction of a particular building type. Other techniques, for example, unit method in certain building types, may be used. The figure will be adjusted to suit local conditions and to take inflation into account. Included in the estimate will be all, or some, of the following:

— professional fees;

— administration and other expenses of the client (for example, legal fees);

— cost of the site and/or demolition;

Fig. A.8 *The main points of three patterns, adapted from* A Pattern Language.

Positive outdoor space
Outdoor spaces which are merely 'left over' between buildings will, in general, not be used.

A

B

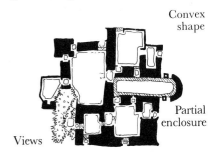

Convex
shape

Partial
enclosure

Views

A. Buildings that create
negative, leftover space.

B. Buildings that create
positive outdoor space.

Therefore:

Make all the outdoor spaces which surround and lie between your buildings positive. Give each one some degree of enclosure; surround each space with wings of buildings, trees, hedges, fences, arcades, and trellised walks, until it becomes an entity with positive quality and does not spill out indefinitely around corners.

Cascade of roofs
Few buildings will be structurally and socially intact, unless the floors step down towards the end of the wings, and unless the roof, accordingly, forms a cascade.

Social entities

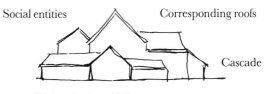

Corresponding roofs

Cascade

Highest in the middle

Therefore:

Visualize the whole building, or building complex, as a system of roofs. Place the largest, highest, and widest roofs over those parts of the building which are most significant; when you come to lay the roofs out in detail, you will be able to make all lesser roofs cascade off these large roofs and form a stable self-buttressing system, which is congruent with the hierarchy of social spaces underneath the roofs.

Intimacy gradient
Unless the spaces in a building are arranged in a sequence which corresponds to their degree of privateness, the visits made by strangers, friends, guests, clients, family, will always be a little awkward.

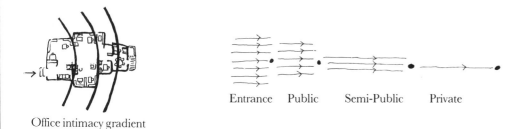

Entrance   Public   Semi-Public   Private

Office intimacy gradient

Therefore:

Lay out the spaces of the building so that they create a sequence which begins with the entrance and the most public parts of the building, then leads into the slightly more private areas, and finally to the most private domains.

— finance costs (mortgages etc); and
— risk and profit element (for example, if the building has to provide an economic return).

It is not an easy task for the quantity surveyor to prepare a realistic estimate as, amongst other things, much depends on his ability to detect the degree of buildability in the designer's proposals. A more detailed estimate is prepared once there is a final scheme design to work from.

— As work proceeds the quantity surveyor will prepare cost studies of alternative solutions, test economic viability, and check regularly that requirements and proposals will not result in expenses that are likely to exceed the cost limit.

— Once a realistic estimate is agreed a cost plan is generally prepared. This plan establishes how the approved estimate will be spent by allocating parts of the sum to individual elements: roof, external walls, wall finishes, heating installation etc (see Fig. A.10). Costs are allocated on a quality basis, usually related to an analysis of completed buildings rather than to specification decisions made for the project in question (these usually happen later in the process). The plan is not a design straightjacket but a framework influencing decision-making and within which the detailed design and specification must be developed. Adjustments can be made as the work proceeds but must be done systematically and under control, so that additional expenditure on one element is balanced by savings on others.

— There are various methods of cost evaluation (not described here), such as life-cycle cost analysis, value analysis and cost-benefit analysis, that may be used to assist in making briefing and design decisions.

Fig. A.9 *Chart indicating basic cost planning procedures in relation to the main briefing and design phases.*

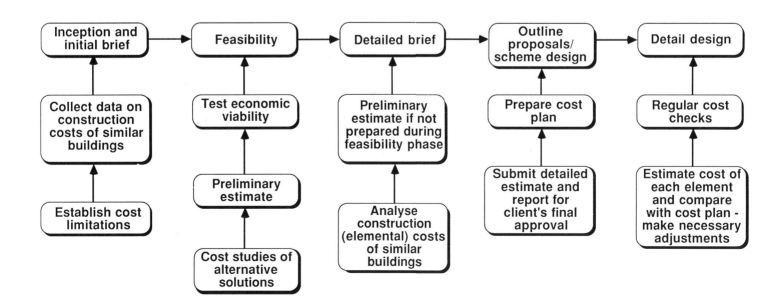

Summary of element costs

	Haringey Central Library		Burnham Library		Central Library, Portsmouth Polytechnic	
	Cost per m² (£)	*Per cent of total*	*Cost per m² (£)*	*Per cent of total*	*Cost per m² (£)*	*Per cent of total*
Preliminaries and insurances	30.17	11.26	17.58	13.75	29.81	15.54
Contingencies	3.67	1.37	11.32	8.86	3.15	1.64
Work below lowest floor finish	24.11	8.99	8.97	7.02	16.06	8.37
Structural elements						
Frame	5.33	1.99	3.80	2.97	7.41	3.86
Upper floors	16.75	6.25	—	—	15.60	8.13
Roofs	14.97	5.58	19.03	14.89	18.82	9.80
Rooflights	—	—	—	—	11.02	5.74
Staircases	3.01	1.12	—	—	5.21	2.71
External walls	13.02	4.86	5.52	4.32	10.09	5.26
Windows	4.88	1.82	} 5.84	} 4.57	15.82	8.24
External doors	0.82	0.31				
Internal walls	4.72	1.76	—	—	—	—
Partitions	1.01	0.38	2.34	1.83	0.93	0.48
Internal doors	3.77	1.41	0.95	0.74	5.23	2.72
Ironmongery	0.99	0.37	—	—	1.07	0.56
Total of structural elements	69.27	25.85	37.48	29.32	91.20	47.50
Finishes and fittings						
Wall finishes	2.83	1.06	4.12	3.22	0.30	0.16
Floor finishes	8.62	3.22	6.93	5.42	2.78	1.45
Ceiling finishes	15.08	5.65	4.01	3.14	—	—
Decoration	3.80	1.42	3.58	2.80	1.58	0.82
Fittings	9.40	3.51	19.11	14.94	6.60	3.44
Total of finishes and fittings	39.73	14.84	37.75	29.52	11.26	5.87
Services						
Sanitary appliances	0.33	0.12	0.42	0.33	0.44	0.23
Waste, soil and overflow pipes	0.92	0.34	0.15	0.12	0.44	0.23
Cold water services	1.75	0.65	0.22	0.17		
Hot water services	1.77	0.66	0.06	0.05		
Heating services	9.47	3.53	4.65	3.64	} 21.05	} 10.97
Ventilation services	59.21	22.08	—	—		
Gas services	0.44	0.16	—	—		
Electrical services	17.51	6.53	7.76	6.06	11.45	5.96
Special services	8.80	3.28	0.08	0.06	6.28	3.27
Drainage	0.90	0.34	1.40	1.10	0.80	0.42
Total of services	101.10	37.69	14.74	11.53	40.46	21.08
Total	268.05	100.00	127.84	100.00	191.94	100.00

Haringey Central Library

SUMMARY:

Ground floor area: 1491 m²
Total floor area: 5305 m²
Gross floor area: 5706 m²
Type of contract: JCT Standard Form of Building Contract Local Authorities Edition with Quantities, 1963 edition. July 1973 Revision with amendment No 9/1975
Tender date: September 1975
Work began: November 1975
Work finished: December 1978
Price of foundation, superstructure, installation and finishes including drainage to collecting manhole (including proportion for preliminaries and contingencies): £1,422,031
Price of external works and ancillary buildings including drainage beyond collecting manhole (including proportion for preliminaries and contingencies): £40,154
Total: £1,462,185

Burnham Library

SUMMARY:

Ground floor area: 577 m²
Total floor area: 577 m²
Type of contract: RIBA firm price
Tender date: March 1972
Work began: June 1972
Work finished: September 1973
Price of foundation, superstructure, installation and finishes including drainage to collecting manhole: £73,764
Price of external works and including drainage beyond collecting manhole: £3,749
Total: £77,513

Central Library Portsmouth Polytechnic

SUMMARY:

Ground floor area: 2037 m²
Total floor area: 3950 m²
Type of contract: JCT contract with quantities fluctuating
Tender date: December 1974
Work began: April 1975
Work finished: September 1977
Price of foundation, superstructure, installation and finishes including drainage to collecting manhole: £758,153
Price of external works and ancillary buildings including drainage beyond collecting manhole: £47,827
Total: £805,980

Fig. A.10 *Example of summary element costs for three library buildings constructed in the UK during the 1970s. (From building studies published in* The Architects' Journal, *23 July 1980: Haringey Central Library; 20 February 1974: Burnham Library; and 4 April 1979: Portsmouth Polytechnic.)*

Conversion Factors and Tables

The system of measures used in this book is 'Système International d'Unités' known in all languages as SI units which are based on the following:

Quantity	Name of unit	Unit symbol
Length	metre	m
Mass	kilogram	kg
Time	second	s
Electric current	ampere	A
Thermodynamic temperature	kelvin*	k
Luminous intensity	candela	cd

* The degree Celsius (°C) is used for all practical purposes.

Quantity	Conversion factors	
Length	1.0 mm	= 0.039 in
	25.4 mm (2.54 cm)	= 1 in
	304.8 mm (30.48 cm)	= 1 ft
	914.4 mm	= 1 yd
	1 000 mm (1.0 m)	= 1 yd 3.4 in (1.093 yd)
	20.117 m	= 1 chain
	1 000.00 m (1 km)	= 0.621 mile
	1 609.31 m	= 1 mile

Area	100 mm^2 (1.0 cm^2)	= 0.155 in^2
	645.2 mm^2 (6.452 cm^2)	= 1 in^2
	929.03 cm^2 (0.093 m^2)	= 1 ft^2
	0.836 m^2	= 1 yd^2
	1.0 m^2	= 1.196 yd^2 (10.763 ft^2)
	0.405 ha (4046.9 m^2)	= 1 acre
	1.0 ha (10 000 m^2)	= 2.471 acre
	1.0 km^2	= 0.386 mile^2
	2.59 km^2 (259 ha)	= 1 mile^2

Temperature	X°C	= ($\frac{9}{5}$X + 32) °F
	$\frac{5}{9}$ × (X − 32) °C	= X°F

Illumination	1 lx (1 lumen/m^2)	= 0.093 ft-candle (0.093 lumen/ft^2)
	10.764 lx	= 1.0 ft-candle (1 lumen/ft^2)

Mass	1.0 g	= 0.035 oz (avoirdupois)
	28.35 g	= 1 oz (avoirdupois)
	454.0 g (0.454 kg)	= 1 lb
	1 000.0 g (1 kg)	= 2.205 lb
	45.36 kg	= 1 cwt US
	907.2 kg (0.907 t)	= 1 ton US
	1 000.0 kg (1.0 t)	= 1.102 ton US

Force	1.0 N	= 0.225 lbf
	1.0 kgf	= 2.205 lbf
	(9.807 N; 1.0 kilopond)	
	4.448 kN	= 1.0 kipf (1 000 lbf)
	8.897 kN	= 1.0 tonf US

Force per unit length	1.0 N/m	= 0.067 lbf/ft
	14.59 N/m	= 1.0 lbf/ft
	175.1 kN/m	= 1.0 lbf/ft
	(175.1 N/mm)	

Tables

Length

mm ⟷ in

mm	in	mm		in
25.4 1	0.04	254.0	10	0.39
50.8 2	0.08	508.0	20	0.79
76.2 3	0.12	762.0	30	1.18
101.6 4	0.16	1016.0	40	1.57
127.0 5	0.2	1270.0	50	1.97
152.4 6	0.24	1524.0	60	2.36
177.8 7	0.28	1778.0	70	2.76
203.2 8	0.31	2032.0	80	3.15
228.6 9	0.35	2286.0	90	3.54
		2540.0	100	3.93

m ⟷ ft

m	ft	m		ft
0.3 1	3.28	3.05	10	32.8
0.61 2	6.56	6.1	20	65.62
0.91 3	9.84	9.14	30	98.43
1.22 4	13.12	12.19	40	131.23
1.52 5	16.4	15.24	50	164.04
1.83 6	19.69	18.29	60	196.85
2.13 7	22.97	21.34	70	229.66
2.44 8	26.25	24.38	80	262.47
2.74 9	29.53	27.43	90	295.28
		30.48	100	328.08

Area

m^2 ⟷ ft^2

m^2	ft^2	m^2		ft^2
0.093 1	10.76	0.93	10	107.64
0.19 2	21.53	1.86	20	215.28
0.28 3	32.29	2.79	30	322.92
0.37 4	43.06	3.72	40	430.56
0.46 5	53.82	4.65	50	538.2
0.56 6	64.58	5.57	60	645.84
0.65 7	75.35	6.5	70	753.47
0.74 8	86.11	7.43	80	861.11
0.84 9	96.88	8.36	90	968.75
		9.29	100	1076.39

Volume

m^3 ⟷ ft^3

m^3	ft^3	m^3		ft^3
0.03 1	35.32	0.28	10	353.15
0.06 2	70.63	0.57	20	706.29
0.08 3	105.94	0.85	30	1059.44
0.11 4	141.26	1.13	40	1412.59
0.14 5	176.57	1.42	50	1765.73
0.17 6	211.89	1.7	60	2118.88
0.2 7	247.2	1.98	70	2472.03
0.23 8	282.52	2.27	80	2825.17
0.25 9	317.83	2.55	90	3178.32
		2.83	100	3531.47